The day I fell, was the day I was....

SAVED

by

Wendy Reakes

Grosvenor House
Publishing Limited

All rights reserved
Copyright © Wendy Reakes, 2015

The right of Wendy Reakes to be identified as the author of this
work has been asserted by her in accordance with Section 78
of the Copyright, Designs and Patents Act 1988

The book cover picture is copyright to Wendy Reakes

This book is published by
Grosvenor House Publishing Ltd
28-30 High Street, Guildford, Surrey, GU1 3EL.
www.grosvenorhousepublishing.co.uk

This book is sold subject to the conditions that it shall not, by way of
trade or otherwise, be lent, resold, hired out or otherwise circulated
without the author's or publisher's prior consent in any form of binding or
cover other than that in which it is published and
without a similar condition including this condition being imposed
on the subsequent purchaser.

All rights reserved. No parts of this publication may be reproduced,
stored in a retrieval system, or transmitted in any form, or by any means,
electronic, mechanical, photocopying, recording, or otherwise, without
the prior permission of the author and copyright owner.

A CIP record for this book
is available from the British Library

ISBN 978-1-78148-362-6

Wendyreakes.com

To Naralyn

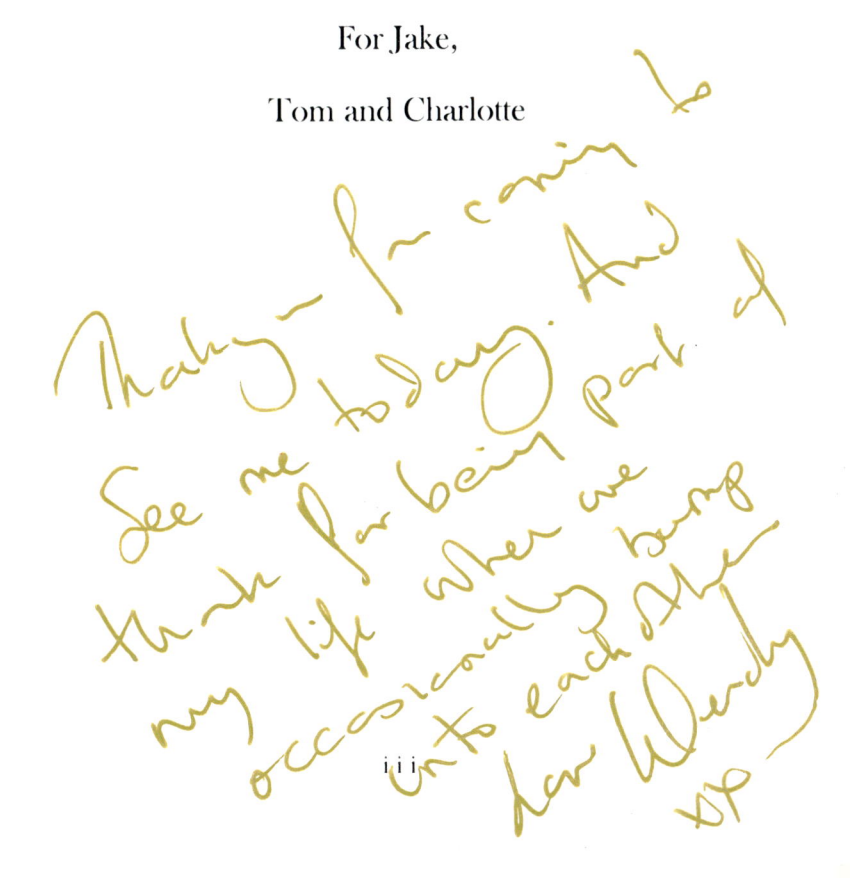

For Jake,

Tom and Charlotte

Thank you for coming to see me today. And thank you for being part of my life when we occasionally bump into each other. Wendy xp

'SAVED is a brave and beautifully written story of one woman's battle against crippling adversity. It is a deeply engaging and inspiring tale of fortitude and faith. It's also an eloquent reminder that from heaven's perspective healing applies to the soul as much as it does to the body.'

Mark Stibbe,
Award winning and bestselling author

Acknowledgements

I'd like to thank *Mark Stibbe* for his support, guidance and invaluable advice with the presentation and publication of my autobiography and all at Spring Harvest, who inspired me to write the book as a Christian publication.

My thanks to my family and friends for putting up with me whilst I wrote this book. Writing novels is easy compared to dissecting one's life and putting it out there in a readable fashion. I appreciate them all for enduring my constant self-doubt and the time-consuming editing of these pages. My special thanks to my friend, Derek, whose new profession of line-editor helped me discover some niggling errors.

I'd like to thank all my church friends who have helped in the transition of finding Jesus (and keeping Him) and I'd like to thank all the people I've ever encountered whilst I've walked this life, for the insight and experience they have provided me with in some shape or form.

I especially want to thank the people in hospital who saved my life and nursed me back to health and I'd like to thank my dad for being there when I needed him most.

Finally, I want to thank Jake for sticking by me every step of the way and my precious twins who taught themselves how to cook whilst I finished a chapter. *That, or go hungry!*

Psalm 139:16

'You saw me before I was born. Every day of my life was recorded in your book. Every moment was laid out before a single day had passed.'

Chapter 1

-Fifty Years of Grey-

BANG, BANG, BANG. I struck that church door with my fist so many times I must have dented it. I was fifteen, naïve and impressionable and I was desperate. I needed God more than I'd ever needed anyone or anything and if I couldn't get inside I'd never reach Him. They had to let me in! We had just received news that my father had suffered a stroke in a foreign land. He was alone and scared, unable to get home. I needed to pray and that door was the gateway to my peace of mind, but it was locked. Five minutes later I left and I never went back. Church was a place I would never again turn to. Period!

I am reminded of that day after fifty years of emptiness and suffering, inexplicable events, unexplained miracles, and the feeling that despite all the tumultuous events of my life, there was always *someone* at my side protecting me. Then in 2012, another church door opened and I at last walked into the light.

Someone said, "You're on a journey."

Yeah, I thought, *tell me about it!*

We were living in a village called Congresbury, a few miles outside Bristol where the A370 fast-tracked commuters into the city, leaving behind leafy suburbs with newly built houses encroaching the green belt, farmland, broken stone walls and hedgerows, and properties featured in Country Life, taking up a whole page, since the price tag offered more zeros than we could ever afford.

Jake and I were renting a bungalow, leased two years before, after we'd returned from a four year existence abroad. That was where we'd spent all our money renovating an old French farmhouse surrounded by its own vineyard...a pool...an orchard... In France our life had been idyllic. It was slow-paced, which suited Jake, but it never suited me. My husband said it was the best time of his life but for me it was one hard slog, an existence I'd spiritually survived alone without support, without a language learning aptitude and with two small children; rebellious twins who viewed their world as one big adventure for them to explore with reckless abandon.

After France chewed us up and spat us out and by the time we'd moved back to England, I had already decided that life was a whole lot easier when I kept myself to myself. In those days, if I could had gotten away with it, I would have built a wall around my home and locked myself away behind a towering iron gate. I could have got some peace there with the stress diminished if not completely eradicated, but the concept was impossible to pull off. My kids had to be run to school and back and they begged to bring home their friends. Peace and solitude was *never* going to happen.

That wretched attitude changed after I slipped on the kitchen floor one day and broke my hip. I'd been frying homemade chips for my lorry driver husband, who even today still claims his favourite meal of egg and chips covered in salt and vinegar could sustain him indefinitely. 'Cholesterol' played no part in his vocabulary and he still maintained a 34 inch waist! Slim, tall and handsome. No negatives required.

That fateful evening, as I fried, a devilish drop of oil spat its slippery-self into my path and I went down heavy, hitting the floor with a sideway turn. Half-an-hour later, I was writhing in agony when the ambulance crew loaded my broken body onto a stretcher and carted me off. They failed to offer me oxygen to relieve the pain, since like me, they'd long ago run out of gas.

A stretch in hospital was undesirable. Jake needed to go to work to bring home the bacon and our nine-year old children needed parental guidance. There was no other option, we had to call in the only person we could rely on.

Jake's mother was gone eighty and she'd long since lost touch with raising children whose manipulating tactics could never be premeditated. On her first day alone with them, they got to bunk off school after they claimed aching stomachs. Untrained in the Reakes children ways, my eighty-one-year old mother-in-law believed them and kept them home. Afterwards she said, "They made a remarkable recovery by ten past nine!"

While I was laid up in Weston-Super-Mare, nursing a fractured hip, the staff at school put up a notice asking for volunteers to run the kids back and forth. *Mrs. Reakes has been taken to hospital*, it said, *and the elderly Mrs. Reakes can't drive*. I had no friends in the village but the school didn't know that. They must have thought the parents of my kid's classmates would flock to help, but that would never happen. At least that was what I thought as I laid back on fluffy white pillows.

I'm not often wrong, but I was that time. I never would have imagined a queue forming in front of the white board in the playground as numerous parents signed their names to assist in caring for Tom and Charlotte whilst I was absent. People with whom I'd never passed the time of day were stepping forward to offer support, and I, in a dark place of negativity, thought the concept unimaginable. One of the people who offered her help was a girl called Avril Chadwick.

-BFF's – Blessed Fated Friends-

I'd seen her many times at school but we'd never spoken. Curiously, we'd often bumped into each other around the village, so much so, it didn't seem natural, as if we were being forced together by some heavenly intervention. We always smiled and said hello but most of the time she always looked like she was dashing around like a crazy person, and I was never particularly interested in stopping to chat either. But as we kept meeting in obscure places, it was hard to ignore the feeling that *someone* or *something* meant for us to be friends. Then one day she arrived at my house to pick up a child belonging to someone else.

My office, otherwise known as an old school desk with a PC on top, was positioned in the hallway of our bungalow, blocking the front door. Avril was looking at the various charts I had dotted around the walls; flipchart pages, displaying clouds, arrows and scribbles. "What's all this?" she asked.

I shrugged. "I'm a writer. This is how I map out all my ideas, research, character profiles, story arcs, plotlines…and so on." I studied her face to see if she was bored yet. She in turn tilted her head to read some of the captions.

"I didn't know."

I shrugged again. "I'm not published yet."

"What are you writing?"

I hate answering that question! I find a quick précis doesn't sound as good as when it's thought through and written down. Nevertheless I said, "It's called The Perfects. Speculative fiction! It's about a magical world underground…under Stonehenge actually."

She had a disapproving look about her. "Underground!? I can only imagine that as being dark and foreboding."

I shook my head as I swung around in my office chair. "Not this place. In the book, survivors of the apocalypse are taken underground. It's beautiful down there – white horses and everything!"

She tilted her head as she observed some of my childlike drawings. "I'm a Christian and I can only imagine it dark…like hell."

"You're a Christian!?" I didn't really know why she told me that. Was she implying my book was anti-Christ? I nodded respectfully while she stared at my facial expression, trying to decipher what I was thinking. At the same time, I was trying to picture her amid a congregation of bible-bashers but that didn't ring true. Avril seemed young and edgy. She didn't strike me as being religious at all.

"I don't like to call it 'religious'," she said.

What did she like to call it then? "I'm very interested in spirituality." I'd always yearned for somewhere else rather than that place on earth. "…but not in a religious way," I added quickly, just in case she got the wrong idea.

She was unperturbed. "I go to a church in Clevedon. If you want, you can come with." *She's South African, so she talks like that. Come with*!

I chuckled and shook my head. "I don't think so. I'm not really a churchy kinda gal," I quipped.

She laughed out of kindness. "You might find it interesting. Our pastor is preaching the trinity."

The kids were running up and down the hallway, screeching and yelling. Any minute now their laughter would inevitably turn to tears. "Okay, why not. Who knows? I might learn something."

"I can drive us."

I nearly panicked. "No! It's okay. I'll take my own car." I figured a getaway vehicle would be the order of the day if things got too heavy!

The following Sunday I took Charlotte with me, seeing as her nine year old brother turned up his nose at the prospect of attending an organised environment. Jake wasn't with me either. There was no way anyone was going to get him to go to church. *No way!*

When we arrived in Clevedon I couldn't recall the name of the church. It had completely gone out of my head. *Why didn't I write it down?* I pondered, driving as if the Highway Code didn't apply to me. *Why didn't Avril write it down?* Charlotte was quiet as we scoured the streets, until I went through a red light. "Mum!" she screamed. "Traffic lights!"

"I'm sorry!" I yelled back. "You try driving while looking for a steeple on an elevated horizon." I checked my mirror in case the police were following me. "There can't be many churches in Clevedon. Maybe we should stop and ask."

"It's near the Curzon cinema," my daughter reminded me. That piece of intel had been provided by Avril's twin girls, Amelie and Grace. They were nine too, so it was difficult for me to imagine the information being reliable, but with my confidence dwindling and having nothing else to go on, we turned right opposite the Curzon and came across an old church on a hill. "That could be it," I said, as we parked up and made our way inside.

-Clerical Error-

When I was a child I had a great affinity with churches. My parents rarely went to church and I was never encouraged, nor required, to attend in any shape or form. However, I do recall a single visit to Sunday school when I was about six. I remember being enthralled by the tales of Jesus and Moses, so I asked my parents to buy me a Bible to read more of the stories that had so enlightened me. It was only January but they waited until the following Christmas to present me with a children's version, full of tales illustrated by colourful pictures. The book was long overdue but I never complained, I was too bowled over with the notion of owning such a beautiful book when I didn't own much else. I spent hours reading it when I discovered there was once a man who loved me unconditionally.

I was a child then and that attitude of reverence was a far cry from when I walked into the wrong church in Clevedon.

It was a beautiful ancient building, full of character and history but the place was only a quarter full. An elderly lady approached me with a booklet. She looked encouraged that two new faces were presumably coming to worship. "Would you like a prayer book?" she asked.

I nearly took it from her but I felt there was something wrong. *Was it the right place?* "I'm looking for Avril," I said with an unconfident whisper.

"We haven't got an Avril, but you're very welcome to stay."

Back in the car, I checked out the clock as I swung around. I was beginning to have second thoughts. I glanced at Charlotte at my side. "I think we'll just go home. I'll explain to Avril when I see her." I pondered that for a moment. "You know, perhaps this is a sign. I don't think church would have suited me anyway."

"Why not, mum?"

I shrugged. "It's a bit boring."

Heading home, we drove past Morrison's and by chance (*or was it?*) Charlotte spotted Avril waving to us from across the car park. I'd almost driven past but I guess God wasn't about to let me go that easily! I pulled in and followed her through the market square into a building that looked like a shop. Inside, people were drinking tea, watching a screen in the corner of the room. I hesitated for a moment. *This isn't me*, I thought. *This isn't me!*

We ascended in a lift to the first floor, arriving at a huge auditorium. Unlike the previous church, Clevedon Baptist Church was packed with worshippers and on a stage at the front was a man, casually attired with his shirt hanging out. At his side stood a large stand-alone wooden cross, simple and bold.

We took our seats and the music began. I'd expected an organ, but in the far corner was a five-piece band with soloists singing lyrics shown on a screen above the stage. The congregation was a mixture of young and old. Children were running about, while the adults sang to modern uplifting songs, some reaching their hands upwards to heaven. The place was rocking! *I mean rocking!*

Avril was swaying her hips in rhythm to the music. I wondered if that wasn't sacrilegious. *Was it allowed?* I pondered...*swaying in church*! Standing next to her were two friends from school, Tina and Tina. They were young mums and they had their kids in tow. *Why were they there?* Suddenly my pre-conceived notion of church being filled with post-war elderly was diminishing by the second.

The music stopped and everyone sat down. Charlotte and the other children were taken away to attend Sunday school, leaving the rest of us in quiet contemplation.

Then it happened.

It was that very moment something inside me changed as if a piece of me had taken root, when the pastor, Rev. Phil Hughes, took to the stage and preached the trinity. God the Father, God the Son and the Holy Spirit. All one!

His sermon blew me away. God had finally got my attention.

When the service concluded, I remained seated whilst I tried to collect my thoughts and the unexpected emotions spilling forth. I had gone there thinking it was going to be a waste of time but within that hour, my life had taken an unexpected and drastic U-turn. I had gone back to my childhood and misspent youth, to the feelings I once had before I became jaded, suspicious and rebellious of the church. Suddenly I was contemplating the life I had led, the disasters and the triumphs, the craziness and the downright ill-fated. Now it was all starting to make sense.

Someone tapped me on the shoulder. "Welcome to Clevedon Baptist church," she said.

I liked her immediately. She had a compassionate and caring look about her, making me feel like I wanted to lean over and cry on her shoulder. "I don't understand this," I said, like a little girl talking to her mother.

Sheila looked puzzled and there was also a look in her eyes I couldn't define, as if I had unbalanced her. "Understand what, love?"

"All of this." I swept my hand in the air, illustrating the stage, with the preacher and the cross…and the blessings…and the love on offer. "I don't know why I'm here. I don't know what I'm supposed to do. I don't know what all this means."

As tears rolled down my cheeks, she placed her arm on my shoulder. "Do you want to talk about it?"

I nodded. "I don't want to be a bother."

"It's no bother. I'll see you Tuesday and we'll have a talk."

I stood up and grabbed my crutches and as I walked out the door, she saw for the first time I only had one leg.

Chapter 2

-Falling to Heaven-

THE DAY WAS JUNE 16TH 1999, the final year of the twentieth century and the day a simple fall changed my life in ways I never could have imagined. Sometimes I reflect on how I almost didn't make it to the new millennium, nor to my impending fortieth birthday. I would never have had children and never got married; I would never have become a writer; and as surely as I sit here writing these words, I would never have found the place I'd been searching for all my life; a place where God was waiting to turn my life around!

At the time, we lived in the North of England. Jake and I had recently bought a property from a piano teacher who'd lived there all her life. It was special to her and it became special to us. Aptly named 'The Nook', the house was situated next to an old church at the poor end of town, a double fronted cream-coloured Victorian townhouse with three receptions and a winding staircase leading to four bedrooms, where behind painted boards the original fireplaces waited to be exposed. I loved that house as much as I loved my job, especially when buying it and moving up the career ladder went hand in hand.

That year I was at my peak; physically, socially and professionally. I had a great boyfriend and we were going to get married one day. I had a top job with handsome rewards, and a very active social life. I was a career girl on the up, literally the epitome of the woman with everything and I'd acquired it with honour and dignity. I was proud of my achievements and I knew people respected and liked me. I'd worked hard, I'd trained, I was a team player, a people person, a motivator. I had contacts in the leisure industry who would do anything for me. I had a name. I was a force. Where else could I have gone…but down?

My career started the day I left school with no qualifications, since I'd missed most of it caring for my disabled mother. I attended Reading College of Technology and studied catering, when, according to my mum, cooking seemed to be the only skill I possessed.

I began life as a chef in the eighties, when female chefs were unheard of. I trained in Switzerland, I became one of the first female chefs in the hot kitchens of the Savoy in London, the *first* female Chef de Partie at Gleneagles in Scotland and I *almost* secured a post at Highgrove as personal chef to the newly married Prince and Princess of Wales. I didn't get the job because I couldn't drive, but I still count it as one of my claims to fame.

In the early eighties I moved my career into pub management. I made financial successes out of several businesses in London and then I sensibly entered line-management as a catering manager...then an area manager... then a regional manager...until I ended up as Head of Marketing of Greenall's PLC in the north of England. The whole process was no mean feat, but that was the type of girl I was. I had no education but I was a fighter and I fought to win.

At Greenall's, my boss was a short, aging Liverpudlian called Bill Link, the bane of my working life. He was also one of the smartest, talented businessmen I'd ever had the pleasure to work with. Bill was an enigma. He was smart and he possessed a whole lot of street cred in the tough Liverpool districts, but he was never an academic. One of his infamous idiosyncrasies was getting the meaning of words wrong, once demanding to know who had made allegations against him. "I want to know who the alligator is," he said. He was politically incorrect to women, sometimes in a cute way and even though he was never a racist, he always seemed to put his foot in it, like singling-out an employee to try the poppadum flavour crisps just because he was Indian. Despite Bill's faults, a big family man, colleague and friend, he had a heart of gold and was fiercely loyal to all who worked loyally for him. I was one of them; one of Bill's girls.

I hadn't always had such high regard for the man who had influenced me greatly during the five years in his employ. When the company I was working for in Bristol was bought out by Greenalls and redundancies were imminent, I was offered the position working for Bill in the North. He wasn't happy about the arrangement and years later he told me he'd threatened to quit if the company forced him to add me to his team.

Back then, clearly disgruntled, he rang me one evening to invite me up north to meet him. "I've already got one female area manager," he said. "I don't really need another."

I laughed. "Thanks. That makes me feel all warm inside."

I sensed a pause. "Well, you can come up on Friday, but don't wear trousers. I don't like women wearing them at work."

I responded with equal fervour. "You're in luck then. I never wear trousers. God forbid anyone would think of me as a bloke. Seems like I'm perfect for you."

Another pause. "Well, we'll have to see."

"Yes, we will." I answered, "And if I decide to take the job, I'll let you know."

I had made up my mind years before that I wouldn't let anyone intimidate me, although my formidable demeanour didn't always work. I put on a good performance of someone in control and who meant business, which was a personal triumph, considering I went through childhood scared of my father. I'd always believed I'd be okay, as long as I stood my ground and showed them I wasn't about to be pushed around. Apart from that, if I had got kicked out of the firm, I was very confident I would be offered a job elsewhere. I was that good! Bill soon learned to respect me for the woman I was, devoted to the business, hard-working and loyal but most of all he loved me because I was sassy and I wasn't afraid to say it like it was. He didn't just love me because I made lots of money for him, but because I also made him look good, since he was the one who took a risk on a girl who everyone else thought of as a pain in the backside and who would probably amount to nothing. Those were the days when a lot of people underestimated Wendy Lyttle.

I'd acquired the 'Lyttle' name from my first husband. We'd been together for six years when I finally acknowledged he preferred fishing to me. I tried not to take it as an insult, but when I realised a muddy river full of slimy carp was way too much competition, we parted with the smoothest divorce in history. The reason for the petition, he said, 'we couldn't see eye to eye.' All it cost me was the price of a stamp. I'm not sure what it cost him, but he did get to keep his tackle!

Two years after working with Bill, an opening came up for the Regional Manager's role. Bill, as head of pubs division, encouraged all his area managers to apply even if they didn't want the job. He said it would look good to the new bosses for his team to appear ambitious. If it hadn't have been for his need to keep up appearances, I probably wouldn't have applied, but like everyone else I did as I was told and put in my application.

In those days, I was a self-proclaimed non-believer. At least that was what I told people. The truth was harder to define so I never chose to. My faith wasn't directed at God. I had faith in mother earth and the power of the eternal spirit and I channelled my prayers towards the dead and the spirits of long lost relatives. I talked to them in the same way I talk to God now but I never really knew if they were there or not. I never had any proof. Not like my relationship with Jesus today, who has demonstrated His greatness to me many times over.

Whatever my faith, that day of my interview I was to find out that *something* spiritual was to have a hand in the outcome. In those days I believed it was the spirit of my deceased mother and brother, there to give me a helping hand. Now, I think it was the 'Holy' Spirit, pushing me in the direction God wanted me to take.

-Adored Adornment-

I was very nervous. I had only been an Area Manager for two short years and frankly I didn't have a hope of getting the job. I wasn't even sure if I wanted it. It was as if I had been led down that path, almost to the point of being forced, and that the consequences were simply out of my control.

That morning, as I was leaving my house, pulling on the jacket of a newly purchased navy pinstripe suit, I grabbed my keys and swung open the back door. Suddenly, as if time and motion had halted, I was made to cast my eyes downward to an object sitting on the middle of the bottom step.

I shook my head when I saw it. I knew what it was, and just for a second I wondered if I was still tucked up in bed, dreaming. There, as bold as you like, sitting on the red painted step, was an old gold locket that had once belonged to my mother when she was a little girl.

I bent down and picked it up and placed it in the palm of my hand. It didn't make sense. I had lost it many years before when I lived in London and I never saw it again until that moment, over ten years later. The whole thing was surreal and how it got there was anyone's guess. My mother died when I was twenty-two and I had no family in the North. Besides, if someone had found it, how would they know where I lived and why would they come along and leave it on my doorstep? Not one explanation made sense.

Inside was a picture of my mother as a baby and a small black and white headshot of my beloved Nan and Bamps. I snapped it closed, shut my eyes and held it against my chest. I couldn't work out how I was now holding that precious thing in my hand but at that moment it had become a lifeline to my future. *Someone* must have known what was going to happen.

An hour later I had the locket firmly fixed inside my closed fingers as I sat in front of four senior executives and gave the interview of my life. Even I don't know where those well-structured answers came from but I came across as efficient, knowledgeable, innovative and determined to make a success of a job I knew nothing about. Seriously, I was oozing so much appeal I must have made their heads spin. At the end of the interview when they offered me the job, I knew it wasn't me in that room that day. It was definitely and miraculously someone else.

The feedback came afterwards, when they all said it was the best interview they had ever witnessed. I thanked them and I was momentarily pleased, until I considered the implications of performing a job I wasn't ready for.

The following morning I met the MD on the stairs. He looked nervous. "I don't know what I've done," he said. "Everyone thinks I've lost my marbles giving the job to you."

I knew how he felt. "Are you saying you've changed your mind?" I think I sounded hopeful. In the cold light of day I was terrified of how I was going to convince everyone I knew what I was doing.

"No, of course not,' he said, "Just don't prove them right."

"I won't."

Before I carried on down the stairs, he called out. "Wendy! That was an amazing interview. Just make sure you do what you told us you could do."

"I will."

And I did. I prospered and grew and I made big profits with my highly motivated team in my one hundred plus, highly desirable pubs.

-A Career Ladder and a Step Ladder-

Four years on, everything I once held dear became threatened by a man, a henchman, hired by the board to shrink the workforce, so that the company would appear good on paper, ready for takeover. He did a stellar job as he single-handily reduced the entire Greenall's management to human wrecks. I was one of them. Suddenly a dark cloud had fallen over my existence and it was only a matter of weeks before I, along with many others, would be thrown out on the streets, as our hard work over the years of developing the company with brands and strategic practices suddenly meant nothing.

But I didn't get fired. Instead, he called me to his office one day and offered me the job of Head of Marketing, since he was going to sack the other one. Apparently I had escaped his 'man-slaughter' because he'd gone into my office when I wasn't there. He was impressed, he told me, to see the walls covered from floor to ceiling with marketing material relating to all the projects that my team had developed for the division; charts, posters, menus, brand logos etc. Most of all, I was out in the field and my desk was tidy. Paperwork done.

When he offered me the job to head up Greenall's marketing department, I frowned at the absurdity of taking on such a role. I wasn't even marketing trained. When I turned it down, he wouldn't accept my answer. After all, he wasn't the sort of man you said no to.

Four weeks later, after the enormous stress of doing a job I never wanted, I asked him to transfer me back into the Restaurant Division as a Regional Manager. He agreed to the move, but I could tell by his eyes my cards were marked.

He didn't get a chance to sack me, because that day in June 1999, I went home with a swollen foot and my life changed forever.

Jake was outside, making the most of the sunshine, as he trimmed the eight-foot high hedge he'd lovingly trained to surround our garden to protect us from prying eyes. "Why don't you come and sit outside," he said, "Put your foot up and rest it." He'd placed a sun lounger onto the lawn and as I hobbled out to the garden, he threw a large towel on the grass a distance away and laid down front-first, sunning his back.

His face was turned away from me when I noticed a wayward leafy branch poking out the top of the hedge. "You missed a bit," I said, vexed by the most obvious exclusion of his chainsaw massacre. He didn't answer. He could have been asleep. I spoke louder. "It's really annoying me."

"Get over it," he threw back.

"I can't. It's bugging me. Why would you leave a branch sticking out of a perfectly cut hedge. It doesn't make sense."

No answer.

I tried to ignore it, but I couldn't. I was obsessed with that straggler and more than anything I wanted Jake to get up and cut it off, regardless of how unreasonable that seemed. Looking back to that day fifteen years later, I can recall every detail but I will never understand what made me climb a ladder that didn't need climbing.

I'm not considered to be an irrational person. It would have suited my character more if I'd looked at that straggler as something that had cleverly escaped the jaws of Jake's trimmer. Under normal circumstances I would have said. 'Good on you, branch. You're still free to grow and prosper to seek the sun and rise...' But instead, I couldn't let it go. I was like a woman possessed with no control over what was about to happen. I was being driven, just like I was driven down that career path with my mother's locket in my hand.

As Jake soaked up the sun, unperturbed by his deluded girlfriend and the branch that had offended her so profusely, I stepped out of character and hobbled into the garage with my still swollen foot. There, I dragged out the stepladders and erected them on the side of the lawn, all the while thinking, *I'll do it myself.*

In front of the hedge was a flower bed with recently turned soil. The ground was uneven but I had no reservations when I placed one leg of the steps onto the soft earth. The other three tottered on the grass a couple of feet from the hedge, which meant I had to lean in. The ladder was unstable, anyone could have seen that but as I look back on that moment now, I must have been on some sort of suicide mission when I climbed it.

I didn't get it at the time but today I like to think of everything that happened as part of God's great plan. At work I was sinking, fighting to keep control over my career, precious to me as life itself, so what would have happened, I wonder, if I hadn't climbed the ladder that day? And now, as I have learned to love God, I have to ask myself, had His divine intervention forced me to take an unchartered route to a place I would never have gone by my own accord? Who knows!

Up on the ladder, with a pair of hedge trimmers in hand, I stood on the sixth step, six-feet off the ground. There, I balanced on one foot as I reached towards the hedge, stretching my arm and pointing the cutters towards the branch that mocked me. When the ladder inevitably toppled, I was finally and unexpectedly thrown backwards into mid-air.

I tossed away the shears in my hand as if by instinct within those micro-seconds, knowing the blades would have hurt me if I'd fallen on them. Then, before I hit the ground, I stuck out my right leg and landed with the full weight of my body above it. With a sickening crunch, I felt the bones of my lower leg crumble beneath me like a tumbling house of cards. I hit the ground on my back, followed by a swift strike to my head.

Jake heard the rattling of the ladders as they crashed to the ground and as he casually looked up from his resting place and saw me lying on the grass with the sun beating down on me, he said "What have you done?"

Jake had often called me accident prone but I really wasn't. I just seemed accident prone to a man who'd never accidently fallen or dropped anything in his life. As far as I was concerned, Jake was perfect and I was normal.

"You'd better ring for an ambulance," I said as I watched him rise up and come towards me, as if he'd only suddenly realised I wasn't joking. I was lying on my back, out of breath, panting the words in a desperate bid to communicate before I passed out from the pain. I knew I would lose consciousness, as I also knew I had irreparably damaged my leg.

Someone told me we can't remember pain. It's true! I can't recall the feeling of it but I do remember it making me feel nauseous. I looked at my leg stretched out in front of me, wrapped in a pair of loose fitting black trousers with my foot lolling to one side. I couldn't see the damage, but I could feel it. I *knew* it was bad.

Waiting for help to arrive, I recalled the impact of my full weight had upon my leg, when the rest of me seemed okay. It was as if my body had been carried on the wings of unseen angels and placed safely on the ground. That notion was made more credible in hospital when no evidence was found of trauma to any other part of my body. Not one bruise!

I can't recall how much time passed before the ambulance came screeching along our road. The only thing I remember from there on was being wheeled past Jake on a stretcher, and saying to him, "Don't forget to lock the door."

So, that was it. That was the day I fell. And that was the day I was saved.

Chapter 3

-Lying in Waiting-

1999

FALLING IN AND OUT of consciousness, I was rushed through town to the nearest hospital's A&E. The place was packed with the injured, all of them hopeful that medical assistance would arrive before the day was through. Jake held my hand while we were kept waiting in a crowded corridor and he appeared more than concerned. In fact his expression made him seem desperate! Afterwards he told me we had been left in the corridor for over an hour waiting for a cubicle to become free so that I could be seen by a doctor. He was concerned about my lack of cohesion and how I seemed to blabber rather than speak.

As for me, my mind was generally calm. Perhaps they'd given me gas and air! I don't recall, but I do remember thinking about my situation as if I was outside my own body. *It's just a broken leg*, I thought, but even though the logic of it was easy to work out, I still couldn't help feeling as if everything was not as it seemed and that I needed all my wits about me if I was to get through the examinations that would surely follow.

I wasn't frightened, I was just being practical. "You can cut away my trousers," I said to the doctor when we finally gained someone's attention. I said it because I knew if they tried taking them off me the usual way, I wouldn't have been able to stand the movement to my leg. It wasn't so much the pain. Somehow, I just knew my leg was wrecked and that the bones were being held together by muscle and skin, hanging there with no substance. I wasn't completely wrong with my self-prognosis. The lower leg had been broken badly, even though I had fallen only six feet from the ground? Today, that notion alone still doesn't make sense, but there you have it.

The rest of my time in A&E was a blur. I have no recollection of it and have no desire to bring the subject up with anyone who may remember. Let's just say I was blissfully unaware and the place I travelled while they poked and prodded, was the best place I could have been.

A couple of days later, I awoke on a ward after an operation to put plates and pins in my leg. I was feeling quite cheerful, as if I'd come through a battle and won. I felt better and I was at peace with my predicament when I saw my leg wrapped in thick white bandages, safe and sound. *Maybe a week in hospital would do me good*, I thought. *Give me a chance to have a rest from work and all the stress that entailed.*

Ward A9 housed eight beds, all filled with elderly ladies (apart from me) who fell in and out of sleep between meals and regular rounds of medication. It appeared to be more of a holding ward for elderly people to be assessed before they were sent to nursing homes, rather than a place for stressed executives to hang out while nursing broken toenails. I don't know why I was there. I guessed they were desperate for beds. The ward had no matron, no sister, and as I assessed the efficiency and quality of the staff (as one does), there appeared to be no one in charge.

"We haven't had matrons for years," one of the nurses said, as she chuckled and tucked clean sheets around my prostate body. "And sister is on holiday."

I was familiar with hospital rules, since my mother had spent so much time in and out of numerous medical facilities. The rule of slippers being kept in lockers at all times seemed to be a thing of the past and so was the usual stringent practices of keeping the ward clean and free of debris. Handbags and dressing gowns were tossed at the end of unmade beds with crumpled sheets and slippers lying abandoned on the stained floor beneath. The standards in existence in my mother's day had clearly dropped.

Over the course of a week I watched the dirt and dust pile up under the bed opposite me. My old boss, Bill, pointed it out when he came to visit. He told me he almost didn't come for fear of catching something but he braved it in the end. I recall his eyes darting over to the opposite bed, where beneath, dead skin and microscopic bugs loitered on the unclean floors. "Have you thought about transferring to private?" he asked.

Under doctor's orders I was on my back for days on end keeping my leg elevated on two pillows. Dozens of visitors came and went and I lost track of how many letters and cards I received. I usually wrote my replies in the wee hours, when everything was quiet. In the middle of the night in the darkened ward, with just an overhead light shining down on my blank pages, I wrote my letters, telling my friends and family how concerned I was about the ward practices. I wrote to my father every day and he to me, and sometimes I wrote to Jake, just to tell him how much I loved him. A never-ending supply of flowers arrived from the company and my colleagues, friends and family, and my area had become so crowded I shared them out with the rest of the patients. I was impressed with everyone's heartfelt words and for once I accepted the love but there was a part of me that wondered why they were all being so generous and attentive. *It's only a broken leg. What's all the fuss about?*

A colleague told me she'd made a poster with my picture on it and posted copies around head office. "Everyone's very upset," she told me.

Why? I pondered. *It's just a broken leg.*

-Pole Hurdling-

While I carried on with life on the ward, a lot of the events that happened from thereon were discussed without me knowing. Jake and dad considered it the best option since my leg wasn't repairing as it should, nor responding to the treatment for fighting an infection. I had no idea that Jake had initially been told by the doctors I would probably end up walking with a limp for the rest of my life. I shouldn't have liked that all, since

I always held myself high when I walked, taking long elegant strides. It demonstrated I knew exactly what I was doing and where I was going. It was one of my things. My mother taught me that.

Then everyone began to notice how my spirit had declined and that I had become unusually morose. It wasn't like me. I was always an up-beat girl, optimistic of life's anomalies and confident that however bad life got, things always turned out okay in the end. I *always* managed a reassuring smile for the people who cared for me but within a week the pain had become worse, despite the regular shots of morphine they used to contain it. I had no appetite and I refused to eat...and I slept a lot...more than usual.

The delirium came then, when I was convinced there was a conspiracy to kill me.

The night staff who changed my sheets used to roll me over, and back again, with indelicate force. "You can't move me like that," I said. "My leg can't be shook about."

My thoughts were frantic. The staff were rough with me when they should have taken more care with a broken leg wrapped only in soft bandages. I couldn't understand them. Why weren't they worried about my leg as much as I? But the more I complained, the more they did it.

As my internal alarm bells rang out and my head became filled with suspicion, I devised a plan to find someone I could trust...to protect me. I knew I needed to stay ultra-alert if I was going to stay alive. So, in desperation, I picked out a nurse called Jane who seemed to have a good instinct with me. She looked like she possessed a high level of control and superiority over the others when she was on shift. With my protector secured, while my health deteriorated more and more each day, I looked out for her, hoping she would stop the others from killing me.

It was all about survival.

I recall my single desire to acquire a monkey pole, so that I can use it to lift myself up when my bed was getting changed or when I was being washed. It made sense, that if they weren't going to take more care over moving me, it would give me the ability to lift myself off the bed when required. Everyone in the ward had a monkey pole, *everyone except me*, so that became the focus of my survival…to get a monkey pole before they killed me.

I thought I was being canny when I targeted Jane above the rest. "Can you get me a monkey lift, please?"

"What do you want one for?" She was sticking a thermometer in my ear.

"It's the night nurses, they keep rolling me over to change my sheets and I'm worried about my leg being moved about all the time. I think it would be better if I could lift myself up for them to change the bed. Stop them moving me about so much!"

As the blood pressure strap strangled my upper arm, she agreed to try and find me one.

But she never did.

I made a point of observing the other patients who were about to be discharged (or died) just so I could get my hands on their monkey pole. I talked to my surgeon. 'They won't give me a monkey pole.'

He smiled and patted my shoulder. Then he passed it back to Jane. "Can't you find her one?" he said.

But she never did.

-Delirious Dilemmas-

When the top of my leg and my foot began to swell over the bandages, the doctors stuck pins in my toes. "Can you feel that?"

I nodded. "Yes, I can feel it."

He smiled. "How about this?"

I couldn't see what he was doing, but I thought I could definitely feel that pin. "Yes, I can feel that too." They offered me compassionate smiles and I accepted them as assurances I was healing nicely. I had no way of knowing that following the examination of my foot, Jake had been told to ring my father. "You need to come up. The doctors want to speak to us."

Dad made the four hour journey from Newbury and Jake collected him from the train station. When he took him back to the house to freshen up, a call came through. It was my surgeon. "Come in straight away."

Half-an-hour later, they were taken into a side room just off the ward. My surgeon looked glum when he dug his hands into his pockets. "I'm sorry to tell you this," he said, "The leg is dead. We are going to have to amputate."

Silence.

Then, "But she only came in with a broken leg," Jake said. "You must have got it wrong."

"It's the infection. We can't control it."

"What about the antibiotics?"

The surgeon's eyes glazed over. "It's gangrene."

Jake was thinking of me as a career girl and how I would react to the news of losing my leg. "I can't go out there and tell her that. Can't you try and save it?"

"We can wait a little bit longer, but we don't hold out much hope."

My father was sobbing in the corner with his head in his hands. He was bereft, as any father would be, but it was no doubt magnified and made more intolerable when only two years before, he suddenly lost his son (my brother) to a brain tumour. Steve died when he was thirty-nine, the same age as me on the day I had my accident, as if the bad fairy had cursed us at birth, preventing us from reaching our fortieth year. Now the news the doctors were delivering went beyond just coping.

That day, instead of doing what they wanted to do, they took me down to theatre to have my cast removed so that they could look at my leg whilst I was under anaesthetic. I was told afterwards they'd performed a fasciectomy by splitting the skin from my knee down to the foot to relieve the pressure. Then they bandaged me up and took me back to the ward.

That night my frustration increased when my leg was elevated so high that iodine was running out of the bandages and down my body. It was in the early hours I asked to be seen by a doctor to make the discomfort go away. A young intern appeared at my side and I told him how the iodine was making it impossible for me to sleep. Without further consultation, I watched him as he simply started to cut through the bandages with a small pair of silver scissors.

What he was doing didn't make sense! I had just spent the afternoon in theatre having my leg freshly bandaged whilst under general anaesthetic. What he was doing *couldn't* be right. Why would he cut off the gauze, in the middle of the night, with a flimsy pair of scissors that only grated through the thickness? "Should you be doing that?" I asked. I was searching his face, to find *something* that would convince me he knew what he was doing.

My fears were worsened by the dropped jaw of the night nurse who had arrived from behind the curtains of the bed next to me. She was carrying an open bed pan as she stopped and stared with disbelief at the young intern cutting away my bandages until my whole bruised and scarred leg became exposed.

The next morning as I was taken back to theatre to have my leg re-dressed, I asked about the incident and quizzed them all for a satisfactory answer to the intern's actions but no one would confirm or deny what he did that night was wrong. Curiously, or maybe not so curiously, I never saw that young doctor again.

That night my delirium took over as I cried for someone to help me. *Someone had to believe they were trying to kill me.* Soon, Jake would come to visit and I'll tell him. Maybe he could get me out of there and into a private hospital. I had BUPA for goodness sake.

I don't know what time I awoke to see another young intern attempting to hit a vein in my arm with a needle. He kept missing, trying over and over again to find the right spot. Surrounding my bed were doctors, nurses, my surgeon, the vascular surgeon…They were all talking about me. The intern missed another vein. I snarled at him and cursed his inefficiency. Then I saw my friend, Diane, standing at the bottom of my bed. I called out as I tried to sit up. "Di, don't let them stop you visiting me. Come over here next to me, Di," I called.

I could see tears in her eyes.

She was upset.

I could tell.

Chapter 4

-A Cut for Life-

PERHAPS THERE'S A TIME in everyone's life when a single day defines them. That day was mine.

The delirium was making me look like I was off my rocker. The accusations I spouted off were becoming embarrassing for the staff and by no means serving as a good reflection for the NHS and its public profile. Heaven knows what I said but it was most probably controversial. I suppose that was why they moved me to a private room and started a daily log of everything I said and did. They must have considered me to be a ticking time bomb and if they weren't careful, the hospital was going to be all over the front pages of every newspaper in the country.

Despite my bouts of delirious aggression, my vulnerability was raw. All I really wanted was to survive that place and the thought of suing was the last thing on my mind. I wanted to live but somehow I knew I was in danger of losing my life. *Somehow* I knew my fate was to die, that something or someone wanted to take me away. But, I didn't want to go. Whoever it was trying to claim me, they weren't going to have me without a fight.

In the beginning I told the staff I didn't want to leave the ward. I somehow knew it was the wrong thing to do and that if I went into a secluded room, the solitude would be the end of me. I had BUPA, I could have easily have moved to a nice clean private hospital with all the trimmings…but something stopped me. I couldn't explain it and I still can't, except for the notion now, that God may have been whispering in my ear in a way that was impossible to ignore. *'Stay in sight, stay in sight…'*

I am reminded of an occasion five years before, when I spent a couple of nights in a private hospital recovering from an operation to heal a hole in my eardrum. It was the middle of the day when I felt a large hand completely cover the side of my face.

It was a healing hand; cool but it was warming too, inside and out. Relishing that loving hand, I kept my eyes closed thinking it was my dad or Jake, who had come to visit. Seconds later when I opened my eyes there was no one there.

-Sarah-

Whether I wanted to go or not, I was transferred to a private room behind the nurse's station, where they could keep an eye on me and keep me quiet. I was assigned a new nurse called Sarah; a no-nonsense matronly type, with a big heart, big bosom and a neat waist pulled in by a wide belt adorned with a silver antique decorative buckle, given to her by her grandmother when she passed her nursing exams. Sara was a true angel in every sense of the word and one who was crucial in saving my life that day.

When she strolled into my room at 9.00am with a couple of syringes in hand and a big smile on her face, she injected morphine into my thigh, along with a shot of antibiotics. "I'm going on my break now," she said as she tucked me up with just a single sheet covering my body. The room was cool, but it would soon get hot when the late morning sun came round to my side of the building.

When Sarah waved me goodbye and closed the door behind her, it was then I began to die.

Drifting off to death was the strangest sensation. The room looked as if it is was moving in ripples but it wasn't just visual. I could hear a humming noise too, as if a gentle tune was playing in rhythm to the waves in front of my eyes. I knew I was going. I'd never experienced death before yet when it happened, I kind of knew what it was.

I became weak very quickly and I lost the use of my arms as if the nerves had become detached from my brain.

I remembered a tray had been left on the trolley at the side of my bed. It was a chance! If I could just knock it off the trolley, the noise of it crashing to the floor would alert someone to come to my rescue. But everyone was on their break, the door was shut, and I couldn't reach the tray with my flailing arms.

I wasn't expecting a miracle but when a miracle stepped into the room at that very instance, it just seemed right. He was simply heaven sent.

Through blurred vision I saw Jake watching me from inside the entrance to my room. His back was pinned against the wall and he was looking at me as if he was seeing something he couldn't process. I panted the words from my flagging lips. "Jake, there's something wrong. Help me." The room was swimming now. I was crashing…falling…

…to blackness.

Chapter 5

-Jake-

I met Jake in very strange circumstances, in August 1993, six years before my accident. That was when I was working in Bristol as an Area Manager for a company called Devenish and living in a corporate flat above *The Steam Tavern* pub on Whiteladies road. It was a Friday night when I went down to the bar after a tough week at work. I often spent my leisure time in the pub downstairs since the manager and staff knew me. It was a home from home and I had no other companionship in Bristol apart from a handful of friends and colleagues.

I was standing at the bar chatting to one of those friends when, without knowing why, I suddenly turned my head to look at the entrance just as Jake walked in through the door.

From my perspective, the room seemed to go silent as my eyes followed him to the place at the other side of the counter, where he stopped with his group of friends out on a stag night. I watched him lean against a pillar as someone thrust a bottle of Budweiser in his hand. He was very tall, 6ft 5, with a neatly trimmed dark beard and short hair that was blond and brown. He wore a dark green suit with a cream shirt open at the neck. He looked so handsome, I fell in love, right there and right then.

From across the room he saw me. I was wearing a nondescript grey t-shirt over black leggings and trainers on my feet. My long brown hair was loose about my shoulders and I was wearing no make-up. I must have looked a mess but I didn't care. As far as I was concerned, the only thing that mattered was the man across the room and how we would end up that night.

Love at first sight! The sensation of such a cosmic event was indescribable. My heart was literally thumping in my chest and my stomach was churning in just the sweetest way. I know now that it was God who gave that to me; such a unique and blessed sensation few people experience in their life time. Even though I didn't know his name, I simply looked at him knowing we were going to spend the rest of our lives together. *I just knew it.*

Then he left.

I saw him being ushered out of the pub by his boisterous mates but just before he went through the door, he took one glance back at me, as if he knew something had just happened but couldn't explain it.

I was devastated by the loss of him. My heart literally ached. He was gone. That was the end of that!

Five minutes later I went to my flat above the pub and threw my keys down upon the table. I slumped into a chair thinking about the man who'd just captured my heart in a single moment and how I was never going to see him again. Suddenly, as if a spirit had yelled in my ear, I stood up, grabbed my keys, shot out of the door and ran down the stairs to my car parked just outside the pub. I revved up the engine and with a ton of blind faith urging me onwards, I drove off to find him.

It was nearing eleven o'clock. The pubs were turning out and hordes of people were walking the route to the nightclubs downtown. The pavements were packed, and the chances of finding him were slim.

But there he was! While his friends lagged behind, jumping over each other in drunken revelry, Jake was strolling along the pavement on the right side of the road with his hands in his pockets. My body was shaking as I steered the car to the opposite curb and pulled over just a few metres behind him.

I was about to call out but I didn't know what to say. I didn't know anything about him. What if I'd picked up the wrong vibes? What if he was married with kids? I was seriously doubting my mentality now. I wound down the window and one of his friends staggered over to my car. I pointed towards Jake walking ahead. "I want to speak to him," I said.

Clearly I'd picked the wrong envoy when he yelled at the top of his voice. "Oi, Jake, there's a bird 'ere who fancies you."

MORTIFIED!

Without any further thought to meeting the man I'd fallen for, I made a drastic three-point-turn and headed back towards my flat. Then I slammed on the brakes. A voice in my head was telling me not to give up.

I knew I had heaven on my side when I turned the car around and went back the way I came. The chances of spotting him for the second time was way beyond any odds I'd care to mention but I saw him once more when he was about to enter a nightclub. If I'd been a second later, I would never have seen him again and I suppose my life would be completely different now.

I screeched to a halt at the side of the road, parking at an abandoned-car-angle between two other vehicles, and just as I switched off the engine, he turned about as if someone had called his name.

My hands clutched the steering wheel when he walked towards me and as he reached my side, without a word, he opened the door. That's when I stepped out of the car and into his life, beginning a love affair spanning twenty-five years.

As for God's involvement, or just those sliding doors, Jake told me later that he had two choices that night. One was to go to a barbecue hosted by a girl called Wendy, and the other, to a stag night with the boys, where he met me, a girl called Wendy.

-Crucial Connections-

Six years on, he'd been at work that morning in June 1999, when just before 9.00am he had an overwhelming feeling that I needed him. "I couldn't explain it," he told me later. "I just knew I had to get to the hospital."

He was working as a logistics manager at a depot in Runcorn, pushing pens, directing men, traffic and cargo, starting each day at 4.00am and finishing at 2.00pm. The two months I was incarcerated in hospital, he had a strict regime of visiting me twice a day, once in the afternoon and then again in the evening. He never deviated, except for the day his granddaughter, Chloe, was born. Each day I watched him walking down the corridor towards me, freshly showered and looking tall, handsome and strong, putting a smile on my face as he leaned down to kiss me hello.

That morning it was out of his usual routine when he suddenly threw down his pen and walked out of work without telling anyone he was leaving. At 9.15am, as I lay dying, he opened the door to my room and saw me on the bed, covered in blood-drenched sheets.

When I cried out for him to help me, he stumbled from the room and went straight to the nurse's station where the male nurse, Charlie, was doing paperwork.

"You need to see Wendy," Jake said.

Charlie was unperturbed as he continued to scrutinise his papers. "Sara's on her break at the moment, Jake. She'll take a look at her when she gets back."

Jake's voice deepened. "This won't wait."

When Charlie looked up and saw the expression on Jake's face, his chair scraped the floor and he rushed to my room where I was *literally* bleeding to death.

As the alarm was sounded and the whole ward became alert to a life or death emergency, teams of medical people rushed to my room pulling in equipment and devices to bring me back to life. It was mayhem.

Sarah had been sent to the blood-bank on the ground floor to collect four bags of blood. She told me afterwards that she'd cared nothing for the patients, staff and visitors when she barged past on her quest to get me the essential supplies. The bags were icy cold when she stuffed them down her bodice to warm them up, and holding onto her mammoth cleavage, she charged through the corridors back to my room.

The blood was fed through my jugular vein at a record rate. They forced the life back into me as they squeezed it into my body by hand. Later they were told, to get so much blood into the system in such a short amount of time was impossible. It had literally gone out one end and back in the other. 'Impossible,' they said.

It took three hours to bring me back from the dead and at one point they told Jake that things weren't looking good and that he should prepare himself for losing me.

"She's only thirty-nine," he said, as he sat in the waiting room in a dazed stupor. "She's too young."

-Doctor Ruth-

I was awoken by someone calling my name. "*Wendy*, come on, Wendy." A terrible pain was shooting through my upper thigh and as I began to wake up and my eyes began to focus, I saw Sarah above me, pressing all her weight down on a vein in my leg to stop the flow of blood exiting my body. I was surrounded by machines and devices and people were rushing in and out of my room while the doctors used their immense skills to revive me.

Later, I awoke again when I was being wheeled out of the room on my bed. The porter stopped inside the doorway as I opened my eyes. I saw Jake next to me holding my hand. I knew I had just fought a battle and that they had saved my life and somehow I knew what Dr Ruth was about to tell me. Her voice was steady and sure when she said gently, "We need to amputate...I'm sorry."

I remember gasping, but I didn't feel like crying. I was spent. I looked up at the man who was the love of my life, the man I wanted to marry and have a future with. "What are we going to do, Jake?" I whispered.

He wore a serene smile when he said, "I think it's a good idea, darling. Afterwards, there'll be no more pain."

No more pain. Yes, that was true. No more of that terrible pain gangrene brings, immeasurable, indescribable pain.

A clipboard was placed in front of me and a pen secured between my fingers. "You need to sign to confirm you give permission for us to operate."

The pen was hovering over the page while I contemplated what I was about to do. Was it the only way?

When I scribbled my signature on the bottom of the form, I closed my eyes at the realisation of what I had just done. They were going to cut off my leg and I was letting them do it.

As the porter pushed my bed through the door, I saw a group of doctors milling about. Jake was standing to the side of the corridor talking to my surgeon as they all watched me being wheeled through. I desperately wanted Jake to hug me one more time, a kiss, or one last word of assurance, but I stopped myself from calling out. I wasn't afraid. I accepted my lot as if it was the most natural thing in the world. I was given strength I didn't know I had, as if God had given me a little bit extra just to get me through the moment.

I was calm on the trip down to theatre, even though it felt like the green mile with something horrific at the end.

When they stopped me in the anteroom, a nurse dressed in a surgical gown and a mask over her face took hold of my hand. She was crying and shaking her head. No words were needed as they began to wire me up.

-A New Awakening-

Many hours later I woke up in intensive care. I panicked when I came around as I felt myself choking on a large pipe in my mouth. A male nurse forced my hand away and removed the tube from my throat. I looked into his eyes to try and see what he was thinking as I briefly wondered if I had dreamed the whole thing. "Is it gone?" I asked.

He nodded. I lifted my head from the pillow and looked down at the empty space where my leg used to be. Below the knee, the sheet was flat on the mattress with no foot sticking up next to the other. It was an odd sight. Unnatural!

Jake was allowed in to see me for just a minute and that was when I cried. I knew he loved me and that even though I wasn't in one piece anymore, his love would never change. *I knew that.* Yes, it's corny, and right now I feel like I'm writing a scene in a soap opera, but, when Jake kissed my hand and asked me to marry him, I said yes.

Later my surgeon came in and stood at the side of my bed and held my hand. He didn't speak. He looked like he was praying for me. He looked wretched. "It's okay," I said. "You did your best."

He nodded and clutched my hand one more time before he went away. And after he'd gone, I went back to sleep, wondering what was ahead.

Chapter 6

-Shirley-

THROUGH ALL THAT TIME, I often wondered how my mother would have coped with what happened to me. Like any mother, she would have tried to remain strong, but beyond her faith and belief that I would soon be well, it would have surely destroyed her inside. Shirley was disabled and mostly bedridden throughout my teens, and she was the sort of woman everyone loved.

As a young girl she was evacuated from her home during the Luftwaffe air raids on Swansea. In the cold and damp air raid shelters she caught Tuberculosis, a disease she carried with her all her life like a burdensome backpack. My dad often said it was Hitler's fault Shirley had been so ill. She was just twelve when she had one of her kidneys removed and she was a young adult when she contracted cancer of the spine. Her spinal operation was such a marvellous accomplishment in those days, that she became a case study in some medical journal or other. She had a scar on the back of her neck, which looked like a zip as it ran down from the top of her spine, there always to remind us of how physically fragile she was.

She fell in love with my dad when she was just seventeen. She adored the bones of him and never stopped loving him, even when he descended into alcohol addiction and made our lives hell. Despite it all, he was the love of her life.

To me, a girl growing up, the memories of my mother were all about death.

Death was everywhere!

My brother was six and I was four when we were woken in the middle of the night and taken to her room where the curtains were closed to life outside. The air was still and stifling and a single lamp shone dimly in the far corner of the room as the doctor packed up his medical bag. Mum's face was deathly pale and she was too weak to move her head from the pillow. Steve was crying and calling *mummy,* but I kept my tears to myself after my dad told us we should be brave and not let her see we were upset. When I reached up and kissed her on the cheek, he took me away again and said, 'That's enough, off you go.'

We awoke the next morning wondering what had happened while we slept. *Was she dead now?* I remember padding along the hall to her room, where I saw her sitting up in bed with rosy cheeks and a smile on her face. It was miraculous, especially since she went on to live another twenty years. And all that time, watching her age, a day didn't go by without me wondering if she was going to die any day.

When my paternal grandfather died, my brother and I were taken to the house the morning after his passing. The adults in those days weren't so hot at shielding children from the tragedies of life. At least my parents weren't. I had always thought of my grandparent's house in Gwynedd Avenue as a loving place filled with family and laughter and childhood games, but when Sam died, overnight it became dark and sad.

That day, my grandmother got out her best dishes and everyone drank lots of tea from china cups, whispering when they talked. I asked my father why all the curtains were closed and he told me it was a mark of respect and a sign to let the neighbours know there had been a death in the family. I remember wondering how long they would stay closed like that. *Would it be forever?*

I was an expert on death procedures by the time I was seven-years old. I knew the curtains should be closed at the front of the house and that doors had to be shut softly. I knew we should all wear black and I knew we should never talk beyond a whisper for days on end. I also knew that a funeral inevitably followed, where my brother and I could munch on delicious sandwiches and cakes and start to laugh and play again.

-Death Sitting-

Yes, death was everywhere.

My mother was in hospital having yet another operation on her spine when I was left with my paternal grandmother, Mam, a wonderful war-time survivor called Winnie, maiden name *Killa*, a name I used for a character in one of my books, *In the Shadow of Strangers*.

Winnie was the epitome of the word grandmother. Everyone adored her and she was the one everyone left their kids with when they had other things to do.

One day it was raining and she had to run errands to the shops. She preferred me to stay in, 'nice and warm,' she said, as she left me with her next-door neighbour, an elderly lady called Mrs. Mitchell who looked about a hundred-years old to a girl of eight.

Within minutes of my grandmother leaving, I was sitting in the front parlour, in front of the fire, reading my Beano, when Mrs. Mitchell suddenly came crashing into the room with her mouth agape and her eyes wide with terror. I was frozen in the chair as I watched her slam her back against the door and then fall like a toppling tower to the floor behind the back of the sofa.

As the room went quiet with just the sound of the clicking clock on the mantelpiece, I dropped my comic to the floor and got to my feet. I sidled around the space in front of the sofa, until I reached the side where Mrs. Mitchell's twitching feet popped out. My mind was on the door as I crept past her but when her whole prostrate form came into view and I saw her flat on her back with her eyes gazing nowhere, I stopped. I was wondering what to do, who to call. *Was it my fault? Would I be told off?* We were alone in the house, as far as I knew, and there was no phone. In fact the nearest one was over the gardens at number thirty-nine. 'She had one,' my grandmother often used to say.

Suddenly a gurgling noise came from Mrs, Mitchell's gaping mouth and frightened the living daylights out of me. 'That was the death rattle,' my brother said later when he quizzed me for all the gory details.

The noise from her gaping mouth made me run out the door, into the hall, where I faced a man standing on the stairs wearing blue striped pyjamas. He screamed at me to go get help, and to tell them to ring for an ambulance. He terrified me more than his dead wife on the parlour floor, so it was without further ado, I tugged on the front door latch and ran out into the rain. I ran down the steps to the back garden where I trampled over rhubarb sticks and cabbages, over the grass and soil and fences, until I reached the house called number thirty-nine.

Yes, death was everywhere.

My Bampa and then Nan, Granddad and Mam, my mother, my brother, my beloved Auntie Ivy, Uncle Ed, Uncle Morris, my best friend's sister, Jane… Death was everywhere. And I watched it all.

Chapter 7

-Sliding Doors-

A STORY IN THE NEWSPAPER told of a local woman who had fallen in a field near her house and broken her leg. There was no one around to help her, so she bled to death before her body was discovered by her husband.

I was shocked by the similarities of her fate compared to mine and I had to wonder if, whatever happened to the woman in the news, was perhaps meant to happen to me, and that maybe my survival was one of life's anomalies, or better still, a gift from God.

God was hardly on my mind in those days. At the beginning, when I tried to find the meaning of it all, my faith could have been enriched by the wonderful and strange events that happened in the years to follow. Instead, I stumbled onwards, coping with the drama with just my common sense and my belief in something spiritual to guide me.

I was changed. I was no longer a woman on the up, and far be it for me to say that the whole event may have seemed like retribution for those who thought of me as a threat. Maybe there was a small glimmer of satisfaction for some who viewed me as a woman who once had everything. A woman now struck down in her prime.

I was never deluded. I knew who loved me and I knew who didn't and even though there was no model for me to follow, no verse from the Bible nor a lesson taught in church, even without those things, I always felt I still had a lot more going for me than many of the people I knew. They may have looked on with unspoken glee but I felt stronger knowing that if our roles had been reversed, I would never have felt that way about them, enemies or not. That was the spirit I had that made me strong. I took their jibes and their cruel words and I banked them. I put them behind me so I could concentrate on living; making my life better and moving forward to the place I was destined to go.

It was a far cry from the place I'd come from.

-Party, Party, Party Fours-

I was born in the sizzling sixties, but the memory I had of my dad's drinking days began in the startling seventies. That's what they were to me, *startling*, a time of fun and partying for the adults, but not so much the kids.

We lived in a little town in Berkshire. Our little suburban cul-d-sac boasted seven modern houses wrapped around a large parking area that branched off to sloping driveways used for the family car. But it was never used for parking, not when each family only ever owned one vehicle. By day it was a play area for the kids to ride their chopper bikes and at night it became a place for a party and a disco with music filtering through an open window of someone's house; *The Hustle* playing from their tape deck.

Young ambitious professionals like my father, introduced the concept of street parties, not just for the purpose of the jubilee or royal weddings. Remember Knott's landing? That was us. Everyone knew everyone else and they never locked their doors. They all went into each other's houses without knocking and threw house parties all year long.

That decadent decade was a time of liberation. The middle classes had easy access to mortgages as they secured good jobs paying more than ever before, giving them the means to elevate quickly through the ranks to higher management levels. It was an attractive proposition at a time when the love of money and possessions escalated from 'making do', to buying what they wanted and building up their company pension and financial portfolio. Liberated indeed!

Sales was the job of the day. Everyone was into it and that included my father who made his money through a substantial salary and commission on top. In the early days he was everyone's bright boy, developing his career through his charming sales strategies and a dynamic approach to company and brand development. He was a winner and he celebrated well, enjoying spending his money on the good things in life, booze!

Alcohol consumption was on the increase. Wine bars were springing up in every town, opening their doors to the ladies for them to meet with friends, dining from a crockpot of Moussaka or a new dish called lasagne, from *Italy* (a place no one had ever been to), washed down with a half carafe of Riesling.

The experience was liberating and contemporary and the working girls loved it. As wine lists grew to include at least four variations, Mateus Rosé became the new wine to drink. It was sweetlicious and after watching an episode of Houseparty (the seventies equivalent of Loose Women) everyone turned the bottle into a lamp. *Some still do!* Blue Nun and Black Tower swiftly followed, until the wine fashionistas turned their pallets to Martini, just because the advert said, '*Any time, any place, anywhere*'.

When home interiors became the order of the day and MFI began to sell impossible to assemble flat-packs, our front room suddenly featured a sideboard, which matched the table. The sideboard was placed in prime position at the end of our modern all-through lounge, where the leaf patterned curtains were closed, to block out the sun from the TV screen. The drawers in the centre of the unit were stuffed with everyone's discarded junk; nearly finished rolls of sellotape, pens that needed filling, a broken zip that needed sewing, three or four paperclips and a safety pin or two, a postcard from Majorca, a bottle opener...And below the shiny red soda syphon next to the giant brandy glass, where inside we kept the car keys, the sliding door on the right opened to reveal the drink supply; perfect rows of Schweppes tonics running alongside ginger ale and Babychams, next to the Advocate, the Gordon's Gin and the ever-faithful Teacher's whiskey.

One of our neighbours was a salesman for Teachers, much to my father's joy. When he wasn't delivering supplies through our back door, he was dishing out dry flat sponges, which exploded in water and doubled in size allowing the Teachers logo to stretch to its limit. (The kids loved those).

In the sideboard dad stored a few cans of that new light beer they called lager, which he make use of only after his first cup of coffee to start the day. By the time he got back from the pub at lunchtime, he started on the Gin&Tonic (or 'water and water' as he liked to call it), and by the end of the day, when the gin was all gone, the whiskey bottle was brought out, no longer in situ in the cabinet but empty at the side of his chair whilst he was passed out in his bath robe.

-Reckoning Reality-

I was a shy, ungainly girl with long uncombed hair hanging across my face in an attempt to conceal my embarrassingly bad teeth. I had big feet, for which I could never buy shoes and I was overly tall -or lanky- as they liked to call me at school. (I was 5'10). It was because of this delightful demeanour and the reflection staring back at me in the bathroom mirror, I preferred to keep to myself. I certainly never voiced an objection or opinion of any kind for fear of being ridiculed, but underneath the layers of my painful personality, I nurtured a certain skill. While I blended into the background, among crowds of strangers or people who simply daunted me, I watched them all and learned about their expressions; a look in their eyes, their personalities, their skills and attributes, visual defects, but most of all I watched their body language. I didn't just become an expert of people's mannerisms and unspoken actions, to top it all, I possessed a gift for remembering places, decors and events, from way back to when I was *very* young. Now I use those skills in my writing as I call upon old experiences of how I felt, or where I was and what I was looking at. It's a very useful ability when developing characters and using visual descriptions. I like to think of those attributes as a gift from God, but perhaps there's a more scientific explanation, since it has been proven that children of alcoholics learn the skill very early on in order to protect themselves.

My father never hit me or my brother. Instead he used mental torture to get us to do what he wanted us to do. And some of the time he wasn't even drunk when he did it.

I am reminded of an occasion when Steve and I and our two cousins were left alone in the house while both our parents went off somewhere. My father at the time worked in Sales for a pharmaceuticals company. His samples were kept in the garage away from our inquisitive eyes since, given the chance, we used to rummage for the white chocolate dog drops. They were delicious! That day, we found the keys and let ourselves into the back of the garage where we took great delight in opening all his samples and mixing them up into assorted gooey concoctions. When he arrived home with a treat of four lucky bags and he saw the mess we'd made, he threw the bags into the fire and made us watch while they burned. In mine was a little plastic black doll with a ring through its nose and I watched it melt before my eyes. Torture indeed!

One summer in the seventies, in one of those street parties that seemed to occur each week, my father's vast girth was bursting forth over his trousers, straining against the fabric of his lime green nylon shirt open to the waist. A whiskey glass in hand and with everyone waiting for the show to begin, his croaking voice rang out and fell on my reddened ears. "Wendy! Come up here and sing the Welsh National Anthem for everyone." There was nothing I did well and I was often reminded of that but in this particular instance, after dad had presumably been watching an episode of New Faces (a seventies version of the X factor), he suddenly decided one of my great accomplishments was singing. "Wendy! Come up here and sing the Welsh National Anthem," he repeated while everyone went quiet and waited for the performance of a lifetime.

I was sitting on a white plastic chair on the un-mowed grass in front of our house when his request resounded in my head and my little danger light flashed on. I turned my torso towards him and shook my head but I knew he wasn't about to let me off the hook. "Come on, Wendy, you stupid girl," he half-jested. His impatience was growing. He had announced the evening's act but the act wasn't coming. "You should be proud to be Welsh," he roared with feigned anger, as everyone laughed. He took a big sniff through his nose and held his head high, demonstrating his pride in his Welsh heritage. "You can sing the National Anthem for everyone." Actually I couldn't. I didn't even know the words, except for the first line, something like, *Land of my father's...* I felt everyone was laughing when his great bulk moved towards me and pulled me off my chair. When I resisted, he stamped his foot. "SING!"

Somehow I managed to break free and run away, holding back tears of degradation until I found a safe place to hide. He called after me. "Wendy! Get back here. NOW!" Everyone at the party was laughing. Or maybe they weren't! I was nine years old and I was shy, so maybe I just thought they were.

-Bombed Babies-

When my dad and the neighbours started running out of excuses to throw a party, they came up with the idea of making them themed. A chip making party (I won that), an Arabian party, Halloween and Valentines party, and once dad hosted a baby party. When eight couples crammed themselves into our twenty-foot lounge, the chairs had been pushed up against the wall and glass ashtrays placed upon the occasional padded seat. Dad was merrily coveting the bar (otherwise known as the sideboard) and food was displayed on the dining room table, protected with Clingfilm, *tight as a drum*. Music was blasting out of the record player which my brother was in charge of and my mum, wearing a light blue crimpolene dress, sat safely out of the way, in her armchair near the door.

One of the games they played whilst temporarily sticking to the baby theme, was for each woman to put a nappy on their partners in record time. My mother couldn't get down on the floor to do it with my dad, so I was called to partner him. I had to fetch a big white towel from the airing cupboard so that I could wrap his large bottom in that. He laid on the carpet in the middle of the room and while I pretended I didn't mind we raced against another couple on the floor next to us. Above, standing in a spectators circle, everyone cheered and egged us on as my father got more and more irritated at my lack of enthusiasm.

I was relieved when it was finally over but because we lost, he called me hopeless and sent me up to bed. Party over!

I can recall so many occasions of my father drinking, I couldn't begin to write about them all. Christmas was the most memorable season. He fell into the tree one year, which kind of wrecked all fanciful festive dreams. And when I was eight he forgot to wrap my presents. I woke up Christmas morning with the usual gut-thrilling anticipation but I found no stuffed sock at the end of my bed. When I went into my parent's room to tell them Santa had forgotten me, dad, sober now, sprang out of bed and ran around the house like the crazy person he was, in the hope of finding an old newspaper to wrap around the few gifts he'd pulled out of the bottom of the wardrobe.

Despite it all, I never stopped loving the man. He was an embarrassment when he was drunk, not forgetting the time I brought home my first boyfriend's parents. He got hammered before they arrived and spent the whole evening half-draped over the boy's mother, calling her *Vera* throughout, even though that wasn't her name.

Finally, when I was fifteen, he came home from work early one day and told me he had been fired from his highly paid job. It was the only time I remember him respecting me enough to confide in me –or it may have been because he was too scared to tell my mother. A 'friend' had reported him for skiving off work and threw in his drinking habits for good measure. Despite the betrayal to him and my mother, it turned out to be a blessing, because from that moment on he got sober and joined AA.

That same year, just as everything was starting to go well and I was at last the happiest little girl in the world, he had a stroke. It was yet another downward turn for our family. He'd become ill whilst on a business trip to Scotland sounding frightened when he called. 'Something's wrong,' he said to my distraught mother. 'I can't feel the left hand side of my body.'' She tried to tell him to stay where he was or to get to a hospital, but he was adamant he was going to come home. He drove for six hours without stopping and all we could do was wait for news.

That was the time when I ran to the church to pray…when I found the door was locked…when I left… and I never went back.

My father often reports in his AA meetings, he stopped drinking the day his daughter walked past the armchair where he was slumped and drooling and she saw an empty bottle of whiskey at its side. He recalls me saying, 'that stuff is going to kill you one day, dad.' From that moment on, he got help and entered the land of the upright and sane. He's been sober and a respected AA member for over forty-years now and I'm really proud of him for that.

Dad. Party, Party

Dad. *Sober days*. The day I was moving to Scotland to start my job at Gleneagles.

Chapter 8

-Cooking for Coins-

I WAS MY MOTHER'S CARER from the age of eight. I did everything in the home; cooking, cleaning, washing, ironing…etc and when I left school with no qualifications, under the circumstances she felt commercial catering was a viable option if I wanted to make a career for myself. I fought her on it at first. *Enough of cooking already*! *It was time to try something else.* But Shirley wasn't someone we said no to. She was a determined woman and at a time when I didn't know what was good for me, *she did*. She made that very clear.

When the day came for me to be interviewed for my college place, I felt pretty daunted when I sat on a lone chair in an assembly hall with a long row of tables on the other side of the room. Five adults stared right at me and the one in the middle said, 'You don't seem to have many exam passes to prove to us you will see this course through." I wasn't very forthright at the age of fifteen, so I simply shrugged. *Well, it wasn't a question as far as I was concerned.* He looked annoyed at me. "Do you have any experience of cooking?"

"My mother is disabled and I've been cooking at home since I was seven or eight."

The panel looked at each other and they were shaking their heads. *I wasn't going to get in.*

I started speaking to draw their attention back to me. "It's plain cooking, but everything is homemade without no artificial additives. We cook mainly roasts and pies and stews so I know how to achieve flavours like using the juices of the meat and the water from the boiled potatoes to make rich dark gravy. Rabbit stew is a big favourite of ours. My dad often brings home a brace already skinned. We soak them overnight in salt water to get the blood out and the next day we cut them into chunky pieces, and simmer them with vegetables. We make our own bread to eat with it. We also make lots of soups and puddings…We make our own pastry…"

"Yes, thank you," the chairman said. They all turned to look at each other and they nodded. I was in.

After two years in college and a stint in a local hotel, I was twenty when I left home to work in Switzerland. It was the early eighties and female chefs were largely unheard of. The very fact I got the job as a chef was a wonder, but employers were beginning to catch on to the new era and females in male domains were becoming the 'in thing'.

At twenty-one I was still impressionable but I was more confident with myself around other people after

I discovered it was important to be polite and nice to them if I was to gain their love and respect. Suddenly I was making my own choices, being my own woman, independent and enjoying life to the full.

I had never travelled alone before, but once again my mother's determination for me to better myself had been the deciding factor. I helped her into bed the night before I left for Switzerland and when I leaned down to kiss her goodnight, she said. "It's time for you to go, my darling girl. You've always looked after me. Go and get a life of your own."

It became a momentous time in my life. Free at last, I was starting my life anew and finally putting my troublesome childhood behind me.

-Alpine Aims-

After a daunting fifteen-hour journey to the mountain top village of Mürren, I stepped out of the darkness of a vertical railway, into a landscape of white and blue and a blazing yellow sun that took my breath away. It was a week before the start of the season and the snow was newly fallen, as if God had sprinkled icing sugar from a frozen sieve. Never before had I set my eyes on snow so white and pure, like crispy meringues below a sky of sapphires. Never before had I breathed such fresh and invigorating air and never before had I felt such a feeling of freedom away from the bleakness of my homeland and the responsibilities that had been a lifetime burden.

When I took my first steps down a snow-covered road with no vehicles to mar its beauty, Swiss wooden chalets lined the way with their roofs blanketed in snow as if they had been trimmed with a hot palette knife along the sides, like frosting on a cake. Enormous icicles, some the size of javelins, hung down from every eave and shutters were closed and doors frozen shut, waiting for their occupants to throw them open in preparation for the new season. Six foot snow drifts lined the sides with small paths carved through them, leading to steps and entrances of fine hotels and boutique shops.

After I walked a mile along the deserted snowy road, I arrived at my destination; the Belle-View Hotel. It was an imposing wooden structure, a chalet-style building with shuttered windows on eighty bedrooms and a restaurant with an external wooden terrace overlooking the cliff to the valley below. Next to a glass-fronted patisserie, standing above a set of wooden, snow-free steps, was a man with his hands on his hips and his arms akimbo, dressed in a white chef's jacket above his normal clothes. His hair was short and black, his skin darkly tanned and his teeth were as white as the snow beneath my feet. In flawless English, with a German lilt, he said, "You are Wendy, ya?" He was cautious when he said something that had perhaps been on his mind for many months before. "We've never had a female chef before, so we'll be putting you in the pantry." *That's the cold kitchen!*

I was used to the whole men versus women thing. I had trained with men who thought they could out-run and out-cook ambitious females and it didn't help, no matter how serious I was about carving-out a career in that masculine domain, that I was an attractive girl with an enviable figure. Burdensome indeed! I shook his hand. "I'll be happy to work wherever you put me," I said, "This is a first for me too."

He was content with my respectful response and as I picked up my backpack once more and flung it over my shoulders, Herr Huggler led me down some stairs and into a dark and quiet basement. In the bowels of the hotel, he opened a door at the end of a long dark corridor, "You are to share a room," he said, "it is another English girl."

A screech hurt my ears when a girl leapt up from one of the beds. She moved swiftly towards me holding out her hand. "Hilary Douse," she said. "Essex girl."

I liked her instantly. She was just a little shorter than me with blond hair and blue eyes, a wide set face and a strangely bent nose. She pointed to it. "Broke it!" she said, "when I was a kid and it was never set right. Terrible isn't it? When I get enough money I'm going to get it done." Her mouth stretched into a wide grin as we shook hands, our friendship already sealed.

Hilary told me she was there for the skiing. She was always bumming around Europe, she said, and she once explored America on a greyhound bus. She spoke three languages, one of which was the essential German and she was to be a waitress in the restaurant, simply to earn enough money for her next big adventure.

My admiration for her many achievements allowed me a small amount of envy. Her head start in that strange place along with her remarkable joie de vie, was something I lacked. I couldn't speak the language, I certainly couldn't ski and I was just there to build a career out of cooking, to pen a few impressive lines on my curriculum vitae. Hilary and I couldn't have been more different. We suited each other perfectly.

On my first day, dressed in my customary chef's whites and a roll of knives beneath my arm, I was introduced to a sixty-five-year old Swiss-German called Ernst; a small, rotund man with a bald head and a high-pitched voice. He spoke no English but his instructions were to show me around the larder kitchen and that I was, in the scheme of things, his boss. "Don't let him take over," Herr Huggler shouted as Ernst stomped off, furious that an English girl, of all people, would be running the place that he considered his domain. Without knowing it, I was pushing him out and he hated me on sight. Herr Huggler offered another retort, and his words reverberated around the dark corridors in the basement of the hotel as if they were ricocheting off each wall. "We will be retiring him soon," he called, as Ernst turned and threw a scoff in our direction, before he entered a room and slammed the door behind him.

Herr Huggler stamped his feet. *Yes, he really did!* "I shall *make him* show you around." He charged down the corridor towards the room Ernst had entered and called back to me as I stood next to the pantry door in my crisp, clean whites. "I'll be back," he shouted.

An old woman in worn slippers shuffled past. She grunted at me when I offered her a meek smile. I was to discover later she was Eda, Ernst's frau.

When I rang home my mother advised me to listen to Herr Huggler and make Ernst realise I was the boss. But I had a better idea.

When Ernst finally restored himself to helping me find my way around the larder kitchen and the workings of it, he was still disgruntled, walking about sulking and pretending I wasn't there. Eventually, heeding Herr Huggler's warning, he went through the motions of showing me everything. One of the specialities of the hotel was incredible dessert concoctions made from their own homemade ice-cream. A machine dedicated to the task took prime position in the larder and one of our jobs was to strip it down and clean it after every batch was made. Ernst showed me once and then twice and when I asked him again a third time to take me through such a complicated procedure, he tilted his bald head and offered me a glimpse of a smile. My plan was working. I figured I'd play dumb and give him back his dignity. By the end of the first week, Ernst and I were brothers in arms and for the rest of the season we worked side by side.

On occasions and much to the surprise of everyone who knew Ernst well, laughter could be heard from the larder kitchen, from a giggling aging Swiss German and a twenty-one year old British girl. And when I sometimes came across Eda, still shuffling along the corridors in those old slippers, she always smiled and said the only English phrase she knew. 'Hello, Wendy.'

My job in the Alps ended after six months of fun, much trepidation, learning German, skiing, meeting new people and learning excellent Swiss cooking skills in the kitchens of the BelleVue Hotel. On the train back to England, I watched the mountains clear of snow as spring emerged and in my hand was a letter. It was confirmation of an interview I was to pass with flying colours, securing me a job as the first female chef in the hot kitchens of the famous Savoy Hotel.

-Savoy and Sunshine-

I looked like I ruled the world when I strolled down the Strand six months later. I was vibrantly positive, and oozing radiance as a new perspective on life took hold of me. It was 1982 and I'd moved to London only a few days before. The Savoy was the most illustrious hotel in Great Britain and I was going to work there. For me, life didn't get any better than that.

I was given a place to live in one of the hotel's hostels in Holland Park where new recruits could stay for the maximum of one year before they had to move to their own accommodation. It was just a room, but it was clean and cheap, and it cost me just £23 a week in a part of London I couldn't have otherwise afforded. I started out as a commis chef on £110 a week and I thought I was the luckiest girl in the world.

There were one-hundred and twenty chefs working at the Savoy in those days, and all of them in the main kitchen were men except for me. A few women worked in the patisserie in the basement, but the hot kitchens were for the tough guys.

They started me off in the poissonnerie where at the end of each day I stunk of fish but I learned how to fillet and prepare all types of dishes. One of them was the art of making quenelles of salmon; little savoury mousses shaped between two spoons, of which we made thousands for banqueting. We started off with dozens of cases of whole salmons, which had to be descaled, filleted and skinned, and the nearly invisible bones pulled out with the blades of a vegetable peeler. The skinned fillets went through a mincer and then pressed through a sieve by hand. The finely sieved salmon was then put into a giant mixer with plenty of salt and then egg whites and cream were added gradually. The only way you could test if the mixture was any good was by poaching one or two. If they didn't stay perfectly formed and if they didn't taste perfectly light, the lot were deemed ruined and unceremoniously dumped. Forty whole Scottish salmon wasted!

A few weeks into my arrival, a new Head Chef started, a native German called Anton Edelman. One day he called me to his office and told me he'd recommended me for a position at Highgrove House as personal chef to the newly married Prince and Princess of Wales. I was honoured to be singled out from all the other chefs and my mum and I were huge fans of Charles and Diana, as were most people in those days before their marriage troubles went public.

The following week I was called to my interview with Sir Hugh Wontner, a representative from the palace who vetted potential staff. We sat together at an enormous, highly polished boardroom table somewhere in the depths of the hotel, a place people like me never got to see. Sir Hugh was very charming and during the interview I gave good responses, until he asked me, "How good are you at keeping secrets?"

"I'm good at it," I said. "But it's my mother you need to worry about." It was true. The whole thing was supposed to be top secret, but by the time my mother told all my aunties, the whole of Swansea knew. The secret was already out!

Eventually the job was given to someone else, a young chef called Chris Barber. I was told, Sir Hugh was very impressed with me, even amused by the reference to my mother but I didn't get the job because I couldn't drive. I didn't mind. The whole experience was a bit daunting for me. I'm sure I would have been too star struck to cook.

There was never a dull moment at the Savoy. One day Chef Edelman, asked me to assist him in filming a documentary for television. It was *The Money Programme* and they wanted to film us preparing a dish with truffles as part of some sort of April fool's joke. There was much excitement at home and when the family and everyone else my mother knew, gathered around the television. All they saw was a quick glimpse of me walking down the middle of the kitchen, where the chef was preparing *Filet Peregrine* with a sauce of truffles. We didn't have a video player in our house then, so it was never recorded and I never saw the clip.

In the second year I was voted employee of the month out of six-hundred Savoy employees and I had my photograph taken for The Savoy Standard, the in-house magazine.

I threw myself into life in London, going to theatres and clubs and restaurants, but my passion was always with The Savoy. I thought it was the most elegant hotel in London. For me, there was no other hotel to touch it, although I believe the Dorchester on Park Avenue came a close second. I tried being nonchalant about working in that fine hotel, but truly, I lapped up the style, history and the splendour of the place. Once, when we were doing a banquet for the Queen, after we had finished serving the 250 guests, I sneaked away from the rest of the chefs and popped my head around the banqueting room door. There she was, sitting so near to where I stood, with her diamond tiara glittering in the light. It was a truly magical sight.

It was the best time of my life working there and I have carried the memory of The Savoy with me always. In terms of the rest of my career, there was nothing to touch it.

-A Grief Pause-

I'd been working at the Savoy for two years when I had a call from home.

The previous week, Mum had admitted herself into the Sue Ryder home in Nettlebed. She told me she was tired and that she was going there to have some rest in a peaceful environment, where she could be cared for by professionals. By the time I arrived, she'd fallen into a deep coma.

I sat with her for just a few hours as we all gathered around her bed and I held her hand when she suddenly opened her eyes and stared right past us. Then she passed away.

No one had told me she had gone in there to die. It was only afterwards I found out she had talked to her doctor about it. She'd told him she was tired of the pain, fighting illness after illness, battling with one thing after another. If I had known, I would never have let her go, but now my darling mother, my best friend in the world, was gone forever. I was twenty-two and losing her broke my heart.

After she went, I felt an emptiness in me that I couldn't eradicate. It was constant and painful and I wanted more than anything to run away. I decided a change was needed so I resigned from the Savoy. The head chef went ballistic, promising me a good future, maybe even a role as junior sous chef within the year. To be given the job as the first female sous chef at The Savoy would have set me up, so I was tempted, but my desire to escape was stronger.

It didn't take me long to find a new post as far away from home as I could get.

-Gleneagles and Gateaux-

I was engaged through an agency to work at Gleneagles in Scotland, as the first *ever* female Chef de Partie (Head of a section). The famous golfing hotel had a kitchen renowned for its army-esque regimes and an all-male brigade of boisterous Scottish chefs and as I toiled among those self-proclaimed alpha-males, they made me face many challenges. The sous chefs were particularly cruel. To them, a woman in the Gleneagles kitchens was a despicable modern approach by the hotel's management and between them, all the kitchen heads plotted to get rid of me.

On my first day, they figured I'd resign by midnight, but they couldn't have known they were up against someone who wouldn't give them the satisfaction! I was staying and despite their treatment, I was going to show them I wasn't just any girl in whites. Of course in those days, there were no laws protecting women in the work place, least of all the male dominated prestigious kitchens. We had to fight every battle on our own and the ones who complained were blatantly asked if it was their 'time of the month'.

It was so bad at Gleneagles, one day one of the chefs grabbed me in front of the rest of the men and planted a love bite on my neck. It was completely humiliating and degrading but I walked away and kept my mouth shut, having to wear a polo neck under my chef jacket for over a week. I never spoke to that chef again and when I sometimes saw him, I gave him a look of distaste, as he snarled back at me.

One evening they all stood around the open grill, teasing me while I cooked over three-hundred rumps. All of the steaks were cooked to order; rare, medium, well done…and they all had to be served within a fifteen minute time-slot. I blocked out the chef's bullying jibes as I concentrated on grilling the steaks, and I perfected them all, *bar one* (apparently). The second chef (the highest ranking to the executive chef), brought the steak back and said it was over-done. They all laughed as he pushed me away and threw on a fresh steak, making it appear as if I'd failed the task.

The one saving grace I had to keep me from walking out and never going back, was when I was scrubbing the grill clean, many of the other lower-ranking chefs each passed my section and gave me a pat on the back. I'd gained their respect and *that* was a huge achievement.

The hotel was renowned for putting on spectacles that were truly breath-taking, like covering one of the banqueting suites in artificial snow to depict a winter theme. Another was a forest with real trees and foliage from floor to ceiling. As I often compared Gleneagles to the Savoy, most of the time I felt the Savoy offered the better cuisine of the two, but I had to admit that the skill Gleneagles excelled at was banqueting.

One of the many pursuits to entertain the female guests while their husbands spent the day on the golf course, were cookery demonstrations. On one occasion the second chef invited me to one of the sessions so that I could see 'how they did it'. I was grateful to be involved, and for a moment there I thought their game playing had finally ended.

Behind a large table stood six senior chefs dressed in dazzling whites with tall hats adding twelve inches to their height. They were an impressive bunch and when they added me to the line-up, all the ladies oohed and ahhed. The chefs began to show off their skills and they lapped up the acclaim from the women in the room. Then the second chef made an announcement, "And now Wendy will demonstrate how to make a *gateau mille feuille.*"

All heads turned to look at me, as everyone clapped and all the chefs took a step back to allow me to walk forward into the fray. Now I knew why he invited me there. It was to throw me under the bus.

As the other chefs watched my face for a reaction, they couldn't have known I'd made many gateaux *mille-feuilles* before and that even though I'd never demonstrated live, with a little faith I could actually pull it off.

As the fifty women in the audience waited for the demonstration of a lifetime, I put on a smile and stepped up to the table. I could see in their eyes they admired me. I was a female chef in a trade dominated by men and they'd never seen one before. They were suitably impressed.

Everyone was waiting, so, on a wing and a prayer, I looked at the table where the cooked puff pastry layers sat ready for construction. The fresh cream was whipped, and the icing was prepared in a shiny glass bowl. I began explaining the process to the ladies with a confidence I never knew I possessed. I put together a beautiful *gateau mille feuille*, demonstrating the art of feathered icing and when it was complete, I was greeted with rapturous applause from the audience. Maybe they could tell from the faces of the other chefs I'd been unashamedly challenged, and that they'd just witnessed me come up with the goods.

While I was being congratulated by some of the chefs for putting on a good show, I caught a glimpse of the second chef who had clearly hoped I was going to mess up the whole thing. He looked defeated, but from that day on, he never challenged me again.

Ultimately, I took a lot of abuse from them but all I ever wanted was their respect so that I could do my job. I think I managed that while I was there but there were some who never recovered from my stint at the illustrious Gleneagles Hotel.

The Glasgow Herald featured my career story in an article dedicated to women in the workplace. *'Her senior position in a kitchen of 65 chefs is so rare, as to be remarkable.'* When interviewed, the Executive Chef Bengt was quoted as saying *'Had I stayed in Europe I probably wouldn't have considered women in the kitchen…Many men are anti-women chefs, but not here.'*

Of the second chef, the article said he was a willing mentor. *'I recognise her talent…If she continues to be assertive she has a great future.'*

-Smart Management-

Adult children of alcoholics are known as over-achievers and that was certainly true of me.

After I'd reached a senior position in the cooking industry, I doubted I could have got any further up the ladder without a tremendous battle. I didn't want to fight anymore. I was tired of having to prove myself all the time to the arrogant male chefs of the day, so just as I was offered a sous chef role at the Mayfair Hilton, I turned it down and decided to leave the industry and try something else.

That's when I started managing pubs in London as a single female manager. When I began making lots of money for the first time in my life, after building four different businesses from nothing to great profit makers, I decided line-management would be my next move.

It was no surprise to anyone that by the time I was finished, I held the position of Regional Manager in charge of over one-hundred restaurant pubs with a team of burly area managers. Somewhere in there I was also nominated for *the Publican's* Businesswoman of the Year Award, coming in the top six out of six-hundred applicants. *I didn't win*, but it wasn't a bad achievement for a girl who left school with one GSE in Art.

The Belle View Hotel. Murren, Switzerland

Hilary and me

COOKING FOR COINS

The Savoy   2nd row from front. 5th from left. Anton Edelman middle of front row.

SAVED

Issue 11　　**THE SAVOY STANDARD**　　September 1983
THE SAVOY, LONDON

Three of a kind

WENDY VAUGHAN (22), second commis chef. She has sent her framed April certificate home to her Mum in Swansea to keep.

Wendy, who has also trained in Switzerland, is outspoken on why she won the award.

She said: "I hope it's for my talents rather than my sex – not just because I'm a female in a job usually done by men."

She has been 13 months at The Savoy, started with sauces and is now on fish and roasts. She likes the work.

Three more winners of the **Employee of the Month** award with the diplomas they collected at a presentation ceremony in suite 515 on August 3.

Employee of the month

After cleaning the stoves

COOKING FOR COINS

The girl's locker rooms. A couple of us had the whole place to ourselves.

SAVED

Gleneagles Hotel Strangely, I'm in the same place as the other one. 2nd row from front. 5th from left.

The Glasgow Herald ran a feature on me being the first female chef de partie. It was such a rare occurrence they gave me a whole page.

Chapter 9

-Misplaced Misery-

IN THE AFTERMATH of the amputation, I enjoyed bouts of euphoria as I found myself very happy to be alive. I rarely dwelled on my circumstances in a negative way, but the times I did, everyone said I'd be in denial if I hadn't. More often than not, I felt energised rather than demoralised.

My days were filled with visitors from all over the country, some of them strangers. One was a lady from the church in the grounds next to my house. She said the congregation had been praying for me. I couldn't claim to be one of their members, so I was glad to accept their prayers. As far as I was concerned I needed all the help I could get.

One of my visitors was the hospital chaplain, who listened to my theories about religion with supreme patience and I'd like to think he may have had me down as a future recruit considering my optimistic views on life and my hope for divine intervention.

Then one day I came crashing down.

It finally hit me like a blow to the chest, when I realised everything in my life was changed and that I would now be reliant on someone else, *forever*. I would never again be the girl I was. I would never be able to make my own choices, I would never be able to go shopping again. Would I even be able to drive? Would Jake leave me? Would I ever work again? Could I ride a bike; dance, go to the beach?

I felt my heart was about to burst with unspent grief, but I couldn't bear the thought of everyone seeing me feel sorry for myself. I needed to get out of the ward to mourn in private. My emotional pain was threatening to burst from my mouth in a spluttering scream as tears were building up, promising to unload like a broken dam. With speed I propelled myself to the dayroom where I was sure I could be alone. I closed the door and wheeled over to the window. Outside, I saw pedestrians walking around the hospital grounds and that's when every negative emotion I had building up inside me collapsed in sheer sorrow. My stomach was aching when I heard someone come into the room.

Dr Ruth was the junior consultant who'd saved my life after squeezing bags of blood into my jugular vein at a record rate. She'd saved my life and because of that I thought of her as extra special. Today, I often thank God for giving her to me at a time when I needed someone to take charge and wherever she is now, I pray she's saving others from the same fate. As I hunched over in my chair, sobbing, I felt her place a hand on my back. "What's wrong, Wendy?" Her voice was gentle and soothing.

I looked up at her as I tried to catch my breath so that I could speak. "I don't know what I've done."

"What do you mean?"

I touched my leg. "This! How could I have been so stupid? Why did it have to happen?"

"It wasn't your fault."

"Yes, it was. I wasn't thinking straight. I don't know what made me climb that ladder. I don't get it. I don't think I'll ever get it."

She was silent for a moment. "Maybe one day you will," she whispered. "I'm a big believer in things happening for a reason. Perhaps there's something out there meant for you."

I brushed my hands over my eyes. "Do you think so? I like the sound of that."

Afterwards she wheeled me back to my room and put me to bed where I slept until evening.

-Emotions Anonymous-

I had many happy moments with my family and friends and my work colleagues who visited in their hoards.

One day my catering team came to visit. They were four young women who worked for me at Greenalls; a gaggle of girls whose own careers I'd nurtured and who were friends more than they were associates. They knew me as Wendy Lyttle, the woman in charge, the one to avoid when in a rage and the woman who gave them all her backing when their troubles took over their desire to climb the corporate ladder.

That day, with a whole lot of personal gusto, they charged into my room like they were running for a bus. There was nothing I could say that would make them relax when they saw me for the first time. It wasn't hard to imagine the conversation they must have had before they came in. 'What do we say? What if we say something wrong? Don't talk about this, don't talk about that…' They'd got themselves so worked up, that when they actually faced me, they were unable to deal with the vision in front of them: Wendy Lyttle in bed with just one leg.

I sympathised with their predicament as I laid back on my pillows. I wanted to laugh and say, "Hey, you lot, I'm just the same as I was; nothing's changed'. Instead, they pinned their backs against the wall for the whole three minutes they stayed. They talked incessantly as if I wasn't there, and finally, when their nerves got the better of them and they could take no more, they rushed from the room in a flurry of suits. Classic!

Almost everyone who came to visit was cheerful. Overly so! It was obvious they were trying to be brave for my sake, as they kept smiles on their faces and chatted about everything other than the topic of the moment: me and my leg…or lack thereof!

Then one morning a very close friend came to see me. I was ready for the usual 'keep-your-pecker-up' talk I'd become accustomed to, but Pauline wasn't able to contain her grief. She broke down and cried as soon as she arrived, mercifully allowing both of us a moment to wallow in the senselessness of it all. Even though she was apologetic for 'bringing me down' I didn't feel that way. I thought her reaction was a refreshing change.

One morning I wheeled myself to the nurse's station to phone dad. I needed something to hang onto, a belief in something tangible; faith in something that had nothing to do with religion. I was desperate for guidance.

Over the years my father's association with AA had given me much insight into how people became desolate without alcohol to sustain them. As far as I was concerned, newly recovering alcoholics were emotional wrecks, not far from how I felt that day. "I wish I was a member of AA," I told him. "I could work it all out with a recovery programme."

Today, I'm baffled how it never occurred to me to turn to God when I was clearly searching for answers. Even in those days my favourite verse was *Footprints*. Whenever I read it, I enjoyed the notion of being carried through times of difficulty by someone greater than any earthly being, but I offered no acknowledgement to God for His part in my recovery. I often wonder where my sense was and why I didn't pick up on the obvious signs that God had provided me with untold strength to get through those days? What on earth was I thinking?

At the other end of the phone, dad was anxious to provide me with something to hang on to, *something* to get me through those first initial steps. He may have mentioned God to me but I chose to dismiss the concept as something that couldn't help. Then I had an idea. "How about stepping stones?" I said. "I can imagine that every step I take could be a path over a raging river with each stone depicting an issue I need to deal with. When I get to the other side, I'll be as good as new."

He sounded relieved and enthused that I was looking at things positively. "I can send you the big book. Or, how about some Emotions Anonymous stuff?"

"Send it over."

The following morning I had a visit from a lady who was my dad's AA contact in the North. Her mission was to give me a talk about how strong I needed to be to face my life ahead but by then I was feeling a lot more positive. When she tried to convince me that despite adversity we can all recover, she went on to tell me the story of her drinking and her subsequent divorce. By the end of her visit, she left uplifted, since I was the one who offered her strength and hope.

Dad called me straight away. 'You were the one who was supposed to be encouraged.'

I laughed. "I felt better by then. I'm using my stepping stones."

The Emotions Anonymous book arrived, a spin off from the big book used in AA. I read the first of the twelve steps. 'Admit you are powerless over your emotions.'

But I wasn't an emotional wreck. I just had the occasional bad day!

Today, much older and a little wiser, I regard the institution of Emotions Anonymous, (used mostly in America), as a poor substitute for a healthy belief in God. I see the rules by which an emotion addict lives by, and to me they seem to be a spinoff of a version of life lessons we all receive from the Bible. It's just a travesty I didn't know that then.

A dear colleague, John, visited me one day. He was an area manager at Greenall's, a veteran, whom everyone respected. In the past, when I was being elevated up the corporate ladder, I had become his regional manager; his boss. I'll never forget the day he was told the news of my promotion. He looked angry and defeated at the realisation someone much younger than him could come in and take over that rung on the ladder which had so far evaded him. He objected strongly, along with all the others, but John was a gentleman and an ally.

That day, he arrived at the same moment I was on the phone pleading with my dad to give me a belief to hold onto. He stood patiently in the wings as he watched me sobbing like a little girl and when I got back into bed, he held my hand as I drifted off to sleep.

When I woke up, he was still there at my side, praying for my recovery.

That was a pretty special moment.

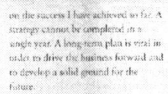

Greenalls

My Catering Team

Picking up an award

MISPLACED MISERY

The Greenall's Oscars

Chapter 10

-The Word becomes Flesh-

I WAS BECOMING SERIOUSLY ill again. The pain in my leg was getting worse as each day passed, despite the morphine they pumped through my veins via a drip attached to my arm. It was never enough to kill the pain that felt like the tip of a dagger was being slowly inserted into my flesh and bone.

My surgeon arrived one morning to unwrap the bandages. Jake was leaning his arm across my body, teasing me about something, trying to distract me. They didn't tell me green and yellow gunge was seeping from my wound, nor did anyone mention the swab the surgeon had taken for analysis. When he left the room, Jake cringed as I writhed in a spasm of pain. He told me later how he could smell that smell again. The gangrene was back!

"We need to talk," my doctor said the next day.

"Okay?" I held my breath since his voice sounded so ominous.

He perched himself at the side of the bed while a nurse stood at the end, both looking seriously glum. "We've had the results back. The infection has spread to your knee. That's what's causing all the pain."

I ran my hand over the top of my leg as the pain intensified. I clenched all my muscles until it passed as I'd become accustomed to doing. The nurse increased the dosage on the IV. "So what do we do?"

"We have to remove it."

I stared into his eyes. "Remove the infection?"

He shook his head "Remove the knee."

"You've got to kidding." But I knew he wasn't. I closed my eyes trying to rationalise losing my knee. "So what does that mean? Will I still be able to wear an artificial leg?"

He nodded and whispered, "Yes, but it'll be a little harder because you'll have to get used to a mechanical knee. There are some good limbs available now though."

I wasn't so sure. "Heather Mills has got her own knee. She can dance and everything. Will I be able to dance without a knee?"

"I don't know. I expect so. We can talk to prosthetics."

When Jake arrived that evening, I told him what the doctor had told me and left it to him to contact friends and family. Everyone was upset all over again.

My father was angry. "Why?" he yelled down the phone. "They said they'd caught the infection."

"It's spread. There's nothing to be done. We'll all just have to get over it."

"When?"

"Friday."
"I'll come up."
"Okay."

-More and More-

I wish I'd welcomed God into my life when they took me down to theatre for the second amputation. If I'd had a Bible, I could have made sense of it all, just as I use it now to make sense of the things that sometimes go wrong (or right) in life.

Unaware of *Him* watching over me, I thought I was using my own strength to get by. I was aware that people were praying for me and I often received little handwritten notes from the ladies in the ward, offering me blessings and virtual hugs and many heartfelt words that meant a great deal to me. I felt so much love from everyone who stuck by me, family and friends and the hospital staff and patients, that I don't think I've ever felt so appreciated in my life before.

The night before my operation a man came into my room. I was lying in darkness, ready for sleeping. As he stood at the side of my bed, a ray of light spilled in from the corridor so I could see his face. He had been visiting his sister on the main ward and he'd heard about me. He was young with a closely shaved head and if I was to judge his character by simply looking at him I may have said he looked a bit of a roughneck but the appraisal couldn't be further from the truth. When I looked at his eyes I felt like I knew how he was feeling, as if he was an open book. He was sad for me, I could tell. He reached out and opened my fingers and placed a small coin in the palm of my hand. "It's my lucky penny," he said. "I want you to have it."

I looked at it in the faded light. "Thank you. That's so...lovely."

"Look after yourself," he said as he left the room.

I thought about him a lot after he left but I never saw him again. I told the nurse about it the next day and showed her the coin. "Can you find his sister?" I asked. "I want to know his name."

"I'll do some digging," she said.

That was the last I heard of the matter. I never found out his name, and after I went home, I wondered if he'd been an angel sent by God to comfort me. I lost the coin and I never found it again, as if it had been taken away and no longer there for me to mull over and appreciate.

-And More-

The operation to amputate my knee was a success.

I was told it had taken a long time to cap the nerve endings so that the phantom pain would be minimal. The phantoms I experienced for many years after were pretty weird. In the early days, if I closed my eyes, I could still feel my foot at the end of my leg, but as time went on, I felt it twisted behind me at a strange angle, which was kind of bizarre. Even today, fifteen years later, I can sometimes feel my big toe itching. *I quite like it!*

The second amputation was a difficult time for my family and friends to accept. They had no choice but to stand by and watch me go through more trauma and heartache and more painful surgery. Jake accepted it as something that would take away the pain and that any difficulties arising from not having a knee would be dealt with as it came. That was the man he was, forever practical.

Two weeks later, I read a newspaper article about a man who believed he didn't feel his leg belonged to him. He'd spent his adult life fighting the system to try and get it amputated but all the doctors he went to refused, claiming it was a perfectly healthy limb and that his problem was mental not physical.

I threw the newspaper down on the bed as my surgeon came into the room. He looked at my glum face. "What's wrong?"

"There's a guy in the paper who wants to have his leg cut off and here I am having no choice in the matter. What's that about?"

"There's some crazy people in the world, Wendy. There's no sense to be made from it. Don't even try."

"Gotcha."

"Listen," he said, "we have a problem."

"What?"

"We haven't caught all the infection. We have to take more off."

My head fell back against the pillow as I closed my eyes. I was tired from the constant pain in my leg, which the morphine had failed to relieve and the idea of a third amputation was seriously depressing. Now I couldn't work on my physiotherapy so I was unable to move forward to get ready for my artificial leg.

My surgeon stayed silent while I breathed slowly trying to come to terms with the inevitable. "How much?"

"Another three-inches."

Three inches! "What if it spreads more after that? If I lose my thigh, I won't be able to wear a prosthesis."

"Let's worry about that if it happens. We're pretty sure we can catch it with this final procedure."

I nodded and laid back on my pillow. "I'm tired." I closed my eyes as he smoothed the sheets over my body and when he shut the door of my room behind him, I sobbed for an hour, mourning the loss of a life I'd never know again.

Chapter 11

-Labels-

AFTER SPENDING eight long weeks in hospital, after three amputations and over twenty-three trips to surgery, I finally went home. To say I was nervous didn't even cover it. I'd become institutionalised in my little private room and going out into the big unsafe world was a daunting prospect. Nevertheless, as usual I put on a brave face as the staff cheered me off, whilst family and friends waited with much anticipation for my home coming.

The week before, the hospital had allowed me home for a trial run but that was only for half a day. Jake had wheeled me out to the car and drove back to the house where we sat in the garden and barbequed sausages on our little pot-belly stove. It was a nice day but it was bizarre too. I felt like a stranger sitting in my once familiar garden and I couldn't help my eyes from darting over to where the ladders had fallen that fateful day in June. What was really obvious though, was how I had become a totally different person to the one who'd left.

I guess it felt like I'd gone back to the beginning of my life, where I had been controlled and looked after like a child. The part in-between, where I'd positioned myself as a determined business woman, a woman who dressed for power, a lover, and a friend to the people who needed me, no longer applied. The cards had changed and suddenly I was someone else.

I watched the people in my life carry on doing the things they did. Getting up to go to work, going to restaurants and pubs, romantic weekend retreats and holidays in the sun. I saw them wear the fashion of the moment, little short cotton skirts and T-shirts, and I listened to them humming Robbie's, *Angel,* a song I'd never heard before, since it had been released while I was in hospital.

Life went on for everyone, but mine was just beginning.

My mother-in-law had turned one of the reception rooms into a downstairs bedroom for me. A double bed took its place in the centre, which meant Jake could sleep next to me. And on a table at the side was a little vase of flowers, put there to cheer up the décor. I often reflect on that little posy as something fresh and beautiful at a time when every bit of my optimism and enthusiasm was being stripped away, at a time when misery came knocking on my door.

-Non-Entitlement Enlightenment-

It's difficult for me write about those days when a dark shadow cast itself over my existence, and I'm reluctant to relive it again, since the gloom of it is not something I relish. However, it's hard to ignore the time when I felt everything spiritual had deserted me. I was lost in a place that was so strange, I had to re-think everything; my personality; my relationships; my down time; how I dressed; and my declining physical appearance. All of me was tested and it took a further three years to work my way through it, to come out the other end in one piece.

If I could turn back the clock, I would change the way I dealt with people who undermined me and treated me as if I had mental problems since I sat in a wheelchair. A part of me rationalised their behaviour, because I was sympathetic to the notion that they were new to the whole thing too, but, there was a part of me that also wondered at their attitude, when it occurred to me I would never have treated them the same way if the situation had been reversed.

They began to talk to me in ways that they would never have talked to me before. They were braver and more confident around me. I was beginning to think I wasn't entitled to an opinion, no right to voice objections, and no right to make waves. I had no defence and no means of attack. I couldn't play the game of wits anymore, since the people I once trusted and nurtured treated me that way.

The whole thing was curiously enlightening. I saw things in them I had never seen before as if they were naked before me and I could see their very souls. But amongst them, my truest friends came to the fore, the strong ones, the ones who had nothing to prove. They were the people who gave me back my dignity and my faith. And thank God they were plentiful.

Strangely, Jake was one of those people who reacted oddly when I came home from hospital. He was his normal lovely-self but in-between, when he wasn't thinking straight, he'd do some strange things, like putting my medication up on a high shelf. It was the most offensive thing to me at a time when I thought I was losing all my independence. I could have self-medicated. I could have kept the pills at the side of my bed. Why was he putting them up on a shelf I couldn't reach? It didn't make sense.

I've just asked him if he thought I was suicidal by placing them out of my reach.

He's just said, "No, it never occurred to me."
"Why did you do it then?" Research!
"I have no idea."
So there you have it.

Another morning I woke up to find he'd locked me in the house. We had latches on all the interior doors, which we secured when we went out, to stop any potential burglars getting from one room to the other. Jake forgot I was still inside and locked them all up before he went to work.

The previous day I had invited my old boss, Bill, to lunch but now I was trapped and the phone was in the hallway, so I couldn't ring him, or anyone else for that matter.

When Bill appeared at noon and I didn't answer the door bell, he went around the side of the house to where my bedroom was. He put his hand up to the window and saw me sitting on my bed. "Jake has locked me in," I shouted.

I felt degraded for looking so helpless and I cursed Jake for being so absentminded. My friend, Di, turned up, at Bill's request and they both talked to me through the window for the whole neighbourhood to witness. Honestly, I was surprised they didn't call the police, or maybe a couple of fire engines and an ambulance!

My humiliation was worsened when I was instructed to get onto the floor and work my way down the steps, through the kitchen and into the lean-to, where I could open the back door. It was an old rusty lock so I had to put all my strength into it, while outside, Bill and Di cheered from the side-lines. Finally I was free, red faced and feeling like the whole damn world was testing me to the limit.

"Where's lunch," Bill said.

-Meals on Wheels-

I'd had a way of dressing before I lost my leg, a certain style. It wasn't brash, nor was it boring but it was mine, and I felt comfortable in clothes that covered me up with just a little bit of sexiness thrown in; a skirt over the knee, or an open button on a silk blouse, it was demure but I carried it off with a hint of femininity as the clothes hugged my slim, curvy figure. After the accident, I had to change all that and I didn't know where to start.

I wanted long skirts to my ankles, but no one was selling them. I wanted flat rubber-soled shoes with peep toes, but no one was selling them, I wanted long tops that covered my thighs, but no one was selling them. And I had to wait two years before long dresses appeared, a life saver and a gift made in heaven. 'God bless the maxi!' *I say that every day.*

In the beginning my clothes were all wrong, I had put on weight, my skin was bloated and I didn't care about wearing make-up any more. I could no longer wear trousers since one leg hung in mid-air with nothing to fill it and I went about in a cheap grey NHS wheelchair. To make matters worse my hair was falling out, brought on by the shock of the accident. My crowning glory was no longer glorious and it took my GP eighteen months of misdiagnosis to set me up with a specialist.

At the BUPA hospital, I was given an answer within minutes when he told me I had an underactive thyroid. By the time he put me on thyroxin, I'd almost gone bald, I'd gone up two dress sizes, I'd pretty much lost my hearing, my vision was dimming and I couldn't wear proper shoes as my feet were too swollen.

As far as I was concerned, all of it was changeable and as soon as I was fit, I would turn my life around and make myself presentable again.

Jake never mentioned how my looks had deteriorated. He always said I shouldn't let it worry me but I'm not sure what he really thought. His practicality and faith in me was a relief since my confidence was waning by the day. After all, most women want to be lied to sometimes.

If my appearance was all that mattered then I could have got past that but my leg wasn't healing, which meant I couldn't get fitted with a prosthesis. In addition, I was now confined to a wheelchair and that wasn't what I'd had in mind for my future at all.

When I found myself tagged with the title 'disabled', it occurred to me I already knew so much. My mother's mobility had worsened as she got older and as the years passed she ended up spending all her time in a wheelchair. I became her carer in an unofficial role, one that was never measured or financed. It was assumed I would do the job, while my father worked, my brother went for a grammar school education and I missed school.

There were few disabled facilities in the seventies. Most people stayed within their own confines and certainly for us, we would never go anywhere without my father checking it out first. If we went to a restaurant or someone's house, he would go beforehand to see if it was suitable; to see if there were stairs to tackle, doors wide enough for a wheelchair and a ground floor toilet. If it wasn't suitable we didn't go.

In my mother's day, the world didn't offer the facilities they offer now. In 1973 when I was twelve, my mother left my dad. I don't know what he did but it was big enough for her to leave him and threaten never to come back. When she booked two train tickets to Swansea over the telephone, she didn't mention her lack of mobility since she was worried they would refuse her. She was right! The trains weren't adequately equipped to take wheelchairs so when we went to collect the tickets, they informed her she couldn't get on.

I stood behind her holding onto the handles of the chair whilst she eloquently and confidently demanded a place on the train. Of course they conceded and said they'd allow her to journey in the guard's van. Waiting on the platform in her chair with her handbag resting on her lap, a porter stood behind her carrying the bags. When the enormous doors of the baggage car slid open, four guards hoisted her in, along with some hearty banter. Inside, they wedged her between the guards own metal chair and a cage filled with boxes and parcels. It was against regulations for me to travel with her so I had to spend the whole trip in a passenger carriage, worrying about my brave mum alone in the guard's van without me to help.

LABELS

My father once took us to a big department store in London. It may have been Selfridges. Even now he cringes at his decision to take mum's wheelchair up on the escalator. The bottom bit was fine. She was facing forward – or downwards, leaning back in her chair while dad tilted it onto its back wheels and my brother and I stood at dad's flank. When the first step rolled out, dad started to struggle. His hands on the chairs handles were almost touching the metal deck and mum was about to scream. Steve and I shoved our bodies in front of the chair using all our strength to stop it crashing to the bottom and all the while we were being transported upwards. We might have made it if someone hadn't raised the alarm and pushed the emergency-stop button.

Now we were suspended half way up, still trying to keep a hold of the chair where mum was about to be catapulted out. We were saved eventually and mum was given a nice cup of tea, but the memory of that went on as something we wouldn't want to repeat.

How ironic, that thirty-five years later I was in the same position, in a wheelchair being pushed around like she, relying on other people to think and act on my behalf.

They say you have to get in one to know what it's like but one of the amazing things that happens is the unspoken relationship one has with the 'pusher', as I had with Jake when he wheeled me about. We had become in-tune with each other and we didn't even know when it had happened.

One of our passions was to hunt around old shops and antique fairs. We'd been doing it for years, always browsing, never buying, unless we saw something we could afford that we just couldn't live without. On our first outing in the chair, we went on an antiques hunt to Salmsebury Hall in Lancashire, a lovely Tudor house that sold antiques and bric-a-brac as auction lots. We were novices and so it didn't occur to us before we left home, it would be impossible to get around a place like that in a wheelchair.

In the car park, Jake pushed me over deep shingle, where we felt like we were in a boat with no water to keep us buoyant. He was out of breath by the time we reached the front door but inside were easy gliding wooden floors and the furniture was gloriously sparse. Our euphoria was short-lived when we discovered the ground floor was a dead end for me.

On the way home, feeling miserable and angry, we spotted a roadside restaurant and pulled in for some lunch. Inside, chairs were scattered about like an invasion of wooden blocks and tables lay before us like an army of predators. The place was packed with diners and as most of them turned to stare, some surveyed the room on our behalf to find a suitable table. Jake and I were both horrified at the attention we were attracting as we inched forward behind a waitress directing us to a place across the other side of the room. It would have been nice if she'd had the foresight to give us something nearer to the entrance but there was no convincing her to change a habit of a lifetime.

When we parked up, Jake bowed his head behind a large folded menu and when he looked up and saw tears welling up in my eyes, he leaned forward and whispered, "Don't do that, Wendy." He turned back to the menu while I mustered all my strength to shake off the gloom, regain my appetite and turn that day around before it became one big disaster.

Chapter 12

-Breaking Battles-

JUST TO MAKE OUR LIFE HARDER than it already was, Jake and I went about building a 24ft extension on the back of the house. Clearly we were gluttons for punishment when we put in a new kitchen/diner, as well as a shower room and laundry. We also turned my downstairs bedroom into a study that could double as a bedroom if the need arose. We didn't have a clue. We made no provisions for me in terms of the future, if I should, *God forbid*, be confined to a wheelchair. I just kept telling everyone I was going to be alright and that when I got my new artificial leg, I would be like new.

The truth was, it was one of the worst times of our lives, seeing as we'd clearly chosen the wrong builders. After much duress, the whole project took over a year to complete and during that time I existed in a wheelchair, propelling myself over cables and rubble with no downstairs loo or kitchen.

I'd been out of hospital for over a week, when my friend, Di, came over to help me sort out some paperwork so that I could apply for some disability benefit and a blue parking badge. I'd been coaxed into applying after I told her husband I didn't need any aid and that I was going to be fine. He was in the business so he knew his stuff. "You're entitled to it," he said. "You've been paying into the scheme all these years, and now they owe you."

He'd thrown some forms in front of me when I was in hospital and I'd filled them out in a positive light. *I'm going to be fine*, I wrote, *this is probably only temporary.* When he read it, he tore it up. 'What are you doing? You have to be more pessimistic."

"I don't feel pessimistic," I argued.

"I'll get you some more forms."

When Di arrived and I was faced with a whole new set to fill in, I went to pieces. It wouldn't have bothered me before but now everything was different. I had changed.

With the blank papers on my desk and just as I was going into meltdown with the pressure of filling out the stupid forms, Jake came home from work. "What's going on?"

I sobbed. "I can't do this. I'm not coping."

"Right," he said with the firm resolve I'd become accustomed to seeing in him. "I'm giving up my job and we'll get through this together."

"You can't do that." *Surely he couldn't!* Underneath I was full of hope that he meant every word.

"It only has to be for a short while. We'll get things sorted out and then I'll go back. It won't be a problem."

-No Frills-

While Jake was at home 24/7 and we were dealing with all the issues of the builders who often didn't show up, Greenalls got taken over by another Pub company.

A war ensued with my employers because of one woman who wanted to take me through the process of applying for my job, just in case I cried 'disability discrimination'. At first I wanted to go back to work, but things were getting pretty scary out there. People were getting laid off or demoted as a re-structuring system was put in place. The woman in charge of my case was passively aggressive, hell-bent on me returning to the role of Area Manager, but I disagreed. My title was Regional Manager and that was the role I wanted to keep.

It was a fight to the death and in the end I won, no thanks to the woman who had dragged me through the process just so they didn't get labelled 'discriminating employer'. They should have just paid me off. It would have been the decent thing to do under the circumstances. From my point of view I had to protect my salary and my pension and all the benefits attached to the job. I couldn't go without a fight.

Early in the process, the Managing Director came to see me. He'd arrived outside my house in his chauffeured limo and we served him fresh coffee from china cups in our elegant dining room. After ten minutes, his mobile phone rang. He chuckled as he looked at the screen and turned it off. "My chauffer was instructed to ring me after ten minutes, to get me out of here." He pushed his cup across the table "Let's have another coffee," he said.

His promise to get me back to work under any circumstances was well met but he hadn't allowed for the vindictiveness of the woman who had been assigned to my case. I recall bumping into him a year later and he seemed surprised I was still around. Haven't they done anything for you yet, Wendy?" he asked.

"Quite the contrary."

The following week I received an offer; a package to get me out.

-Blood and guts-

As I was fighting the legal battle at work, I picked up another infection in my leg that gave me constant, agonising pain. A shard of bone was loose inside, travelling and ripping through my flesh as my body tried to reject it. There was no other option, I had to have another operation.

At short notice they made a bed available in the ward next to the one I'd spent three months in. Beds were in short supply, so they wheeled me down to the far end of the ward and put me into a private room. When I looked down, I was faced with a huge red patch staining the middle of the carpet tiles. Old blood! I got up out of my wheelchair and moved onto the bed, covering my leg to keep it away from any germs in the air. The nurse came back and I pointed to the stain "Is that blood?"

She shrugged. "Yes, it needs cleaning."

"I can't stay here. I'm sorry. I haven't complained much about the hygiene in the past but enough is enough. I want to be moved out of this room right now."

"The only other place where we can put your bed would be in the visitor's room."

Seriously!? "But that has carpet too, hasn't it?" I couldn't even begin to imagine the germs in it. "Why would you even have it?"

"Costs!"

I made so much fuss, they had no choice but to swap me around with another patient who was unlucky enough to have the *bloody* floor.

After the operation to remove the shard of bone, one of my surgeon's team came to change my dressings. He was very talkative, acting as if he enjoyed boasting about his medical prowess. I didn't care for him much. He was too much of a show off for me. I disliked him more when he began to run away with himself. He told me that the MRSA infection inside my leg would never go away and that I would carry it around with me for the rest of my life. He looked up whilst still fiddling with the bandages and saw a frown on my face.

"MRSA?" I asked with a drawn out tone to my voice.

The nurse assisting him darted off, whilst he continued chattering, unperturbed to the danger of providing me with too much information. "It's the new superbug going around the NHS hospitals," he explained "Once you're got it you'll never get rid of it".

I never saw that young doctor again. He was probably sent back to school with the other one.

-Better legs-

As the infection continued, despite the shard of bone being removed, I was making regular trips to the hospital where I was seen by my surgeon in the outpatients department. They told me there was a chance I could lose more of my leg but they wanted to try a drain first. They put me on strong antibiotics and inserted a tube through the wound that seeped green and yellow puss. All the while I had regular visits to Clatterbridge Hospital on the Wirral, to the amputee clinic where I had to do regular exercises before I could take a prosthesis.

Initially, while I was still in hospital, I was encouraged to go to the hospital gym to get my residual limb ready for my new leg. Despite my keenness to get started, it wasn't just something you slipped on and ran with. Firstly, I had to build up my muscles and then I had to practice the art of walking, after I had gone through the process of the leg being made to fit me like a glove.

That's when I met the doctor in charge of the amputee clinic whose bedside manner was not as adept as his knowledge of prosthetics, since he had an obvious bias against women regardless of their age or capabilities.

Every Tuesday he used to sit inside a small cubicle with a curtain dividing him from the amputee patients waiting in line to see him. The first time I went, I was wheeled into his little cupboard (as I called it) where he didn't look at me once. Instead he spoke to Jake. "Get her up onto the bed."

His approach was offensive and completely archaic, but faced with the absurdity of the situation, Jake and I exchanged glances and willed each other not to laugh, when it wasn't easy not to. While Jake stood to one side, I got up from my wheelchair and shifted my body onto the bed, trying hard to contain a bout of the giggles. Meanwhile the doctor kept his eyes on his clipboard as he pulled out his tape measure and started measuring what was left of my leg. He muttered to himself as he jotted down the dimensions and when he was finished, he dismissed me without a by-your-leave.

The experience didn't leave me with a lot of confidence in the system, until I was assigned a proper, more youthful prosthetist called Ken. While the other doctor was someone to avoid at all cost, Ken was a blessing. He was smart and innovative, a forward thinker, kind, gentle and totally appreciative of my needs. I thanked God for him.

I met Ken when I first lost my leg. He came to the gym one day to talk to me about the future. He was tall, Scottish, about the same age as me and he had a very confident air about him. I liked him immediately. He worked for Blatchford's Prosthetics but he was based at Clatterbridge Hospital, heading up the limb centre and its team. There wasn't much he didn't know about artificial legs and when he assured me he would soon get me walking again, I knew I was in good hands. I called him 'my leg man' and he was the best thing that happened to me at a time when I was desperate for someone to take charge.

Ken was my light at the end of the tunnel. He kept up with new innovations and new products on the market and if he hadn't been on courses on how to motivate his patients and to see a job through, he was born with the art. He had a passion for his trade and the people he was treating. He would push the system to its limits and take advantage of every facility there was, just so he could give them the best that was on the market, within reason.

He said "Don't ask me for a leg that you can use to play tennis, when you've never played tennis before."

He was firm and very direct and even though he didn't discuss his plans for me, I knew he had something up his sleeve. I wasn't one of his normal patients. He knew I was still young and that I had years of normal health and activity ahead of me. He had to give me something that would give me back the life I once had, to make me normal again.

Ken fought the system on my behalf, to give me a higher grade leg, normally only provided for war casualties or private patients.

All the other women in the clinic were a lot older than me. Most of them had lost their limbs to illnesses like diabetes but the younger ones, who maintained an independent spirit, Ken did everything he could to get us decent legs.

In my case, after I was given my super-duper leg, they covered it in a piece of foam and pulled an orange stocking over it, since skin-effect coverings weren't available on the NHS. I had a good knee joint to enable me to walk well but the cosmetic appearance looked dire. The foot was a lump of plastic with moulded toes, so I couldn't wear sandals, nor was it adjustable, so I couldn't wear heels. Looking down at my feet was a constant source of embarrassment, as everyone compared the real one with the one that didn't belong to me and more often than not they frowned.

I could have gone private to the clinic in Dorset where Heather Mills went but I was quoted £23,000 for a leg that would need replacing within two years, so it wasn't a viable option. Instead I stuck with the NHS, hoping, and constantly nagging for a decent skin-effect covering, which would allow me to walk outside without being stared at all the time.

-Last leg-

Finally, one day I took matters into my own hands. I took some scissors, glue and a shampoo bottle and created my own toenails. False ones from the shop were no good as they were usually fingernails and not wide enough for the toes of a man's artificial foot; a man's foot, because I take a size eight shoe and they didn't go up that big for a woman. That day I cut out nail shapes from the shampoo bottle and glued them over the toes of the plastic man-foot, painting them dark pink. They looked okay at the beginning so I wore sandals that day, until the nails started falling off.

When I relayed the story to the Clatterbridge team, hoping to make a point, they congratulated me on my ingenuity but that wasn't the response I was looking for. I asked them if I had lost a breast would they have expected me to make my own nipples.

They gave me a skin effect cover after that; anything to keep me quiet. It was a nice offer but the toes still weren't defined, so I continued to wear closed-toe shoes all year round.

The reaction I had from strangers when I went out was mixed. Most of them glanced at me and then quickly looked away but I had a few funny incidents from the younger set.

I was wheeling myself around a department store when I saw a woman walk down the aisle towards me holding the hand of a little girl of about six or seven. Just as they got closer the little girl said, "Mummy, why has that lady only got one leg?" The woman averted her eyes and carried on walking past but the child wasn't happy about her mother's discreet silence. She repeated the question and said it louder. "Mummy," she yelled, "why has that lady only got one leg?" When I stopped and turned about with a smile on my face, the little girl's mother looked like she wanted to crawl into a hole. "I'm sorry," she mouthed, before she dragged off her daughter who was still demanding a reply.

Another time, some friends came over to the house for dinner. I didn't have to be a genius to work out they had told their two young daughters not to say anything about my leg. I watched them all evening as they avoided speaking about it, but in the end they just couldn't help themselves. With their mother out of earshot, they followed me into a room and closed the door behind them. Then they both confronted me. "Wendy, what happened to your leg?"

That's what I love about kids. They have nothing to hide and they say it like it is.

When I finally took ownership of my leg, the cosmetic appearance was the least of my problems. After much pain and heartache over a period of two years, I had finally got a payoff from the company and was let go. It was the result I'd been waiting for, because Jake and I had plans. Big plans!

END OF PART 1

PART 2

I have discovered while writing these memoirs, that despite all the challenges I once faced, I wouldn't have had the wonderful life I have now if I hadn't have lost my leg.

A number of people have asked me why I didn't sue the hospital but I seek no retribution for the treatment I received. I believe the whole episode was meant to be.

Despite the loss of my mobility, the excellent doctors and staff saved my life, so I would never have gone up against them with legal proceedings. As far as I'm concerned they were let down by the system and the government who denied them proper funding.

I have tried to exclude any names from this account, to protect the hospital and its staff. I have just wanted to tell my story, rather than try to persecute the people who helped me. Besides, the hospital has had a big makeover since my time there, so no one else has anything to worry about.

Now that I've found God, I reflect on the whole episode as being a necessary turnaround for a woman who had much more to offer than just a career. I like to think it was God's will for me to travel that road to be at His side. He's been calling me all my life but I didn't listen. Maybe He needed to take drastic action to make me hear. Who knows!

Despite it all, I'm grateful for the rewards He's given me to make up for all that hardship and I am thankful He was there to pick me up every time I fell.

Hold that thought, because in the rest of this book I'm going to demonstrate how many more strange events happened that were so well-timed, only heavenly intervention could have had a hand in them.

As my friend, Avril, once said, 'there are no coincidences with God.'

Wendy

Chapter 13

-No means Yes-

The single thing that remained constant over the years was the love I felt for the man in my life, Jake. He was my rock; one that every woman should have. He saved me in more ways I can remember, giving me so much and wanting so little in return. When I was in hospital, between his visits -twice a day without fail- he held down a job, cleaned our home, washed and ironed clothes and talked to dozens of family and friends on the phone every night. He was my mental and physical support and he never faltered in his love for me. The whole episode truly was Jake Reakes' finest hour.

We'd talked about having children long before I lost my leg. Before then, I always felt I was never ready to start a family since my job was my main goal in life. Jake said he wanted the mother of his children to be at home, not out working each day while they were raised by child minders. "You're so old fashioned." I argued. "Women don't stay at home any more. Not since Noah!" We never did agree!

When the work on the house was finished, Jake brought up the subject again. "We could try for a baby now," he said. "You're not working. Our lives are a blank page to write on." Suddenly we were excited about the prospect of increasing our family, only after we discussed the whole thing in detail about how I was going to manage. "Other women have done it," Jake said. "I know you can too."

Six months later, when I still wasn't pregnant, we decided to get checked out. It turned out the fault was mine, while Jake on the other hand was capable of fathering babies for the whole of Manchester – at least that was how the doctor put it, as Jake nodded with immense pride.

The IVF route was our next step and if ever there was a miracle, this one was for keeps. It wasn't just a miracle of science nor one of your ordinary run-of-the-mill miracles, this was a heavenly gift, just like the time I met Jake when, no matter what, God meant for us to succeed despite such small odds.

We registered with a private clinic in Manchester and put enough aside for three rounds of IVF at four thousand a pop. Our treatment was scheduled to start the following week and we were raring to go.

The injections were kind of fun. They didn't hurt, seeing as Jake had practised on a full bowl of oranges before I let him near me. He was pretty adept, except for the occasions when we had one of our two-minute fights. For some reason those hurt!

We kept our plans to ourselves. We didn't want anyone's interference at a time when everyone had something to say about how our lives should be. It was for Jake and I only, as something we could achieve without the rest of the world knowing about it.

After the first round of treatment, the doctors advised us not to take a pregnancy test until the 14th day. I was adamant I was going to stick by that, in case the test came up negative. I was happier living in a land of deluded happiness until the very last.

The morning I was due to take the test, I was pretty optimistic but I couldn't bear to look at it myself. I asked Jake to watch the blue line appear but when his face dropped, I knew it was negative. I wasn't pregnant.

It was another life blow that made the colour of my mood turn to dark grey.

It was a Sunday and it was sunny outside, so Jake ushered me out of the house to the car to go to an antique fair. Those were the days when they were plentiful. Ebay wasn't even a twinkle in someone's eye and car boot sales actually sold everyone's junk, rather than trader's peddling their wares. It was easy to pick up a picture, or an ornament of some worth since no one knew the value of what they were selling.

That day there was an antique fair at Tatton Park, a beautiful old Manor house near Manchester airport. "We'll just go and have a mosie," Jake said from the driving seat as I stared out of the window on the other side, watching the clouds shade the sun and the rain begin. The weather suited my mood. I was fed up with life.

Self-pity has always been something I avoided without having to try too hard. My optimistic view that problems weren't problems, only opportunities for improvement, was the very thing that kept me going during those years. I was almost always upbeat but that day, I started to wonder if I was just plain stupid to believe in someone up there guiding me.

To reiterate, I never thought of it being God. In those days it was simply a kindly spirit, which remained undefined up until I finally discovered Jesus ten years later.

-Believing Buddha-

Jake and I walked around the antiques show hand in hand until he found a picture stand and went off alone. My heart was heavy and even the beautiful furniture couldn't sway me from my miserable state of mind. I was wearing my artificial leg and walking with a stick. My eyes were red and puffy and I wore a permanently fixed frown on my face. Then, just as Jake found his way back to me, I spotted a stall that sold Buddha figurines. "Buddhas!" I chanted, as I headed towards the stall with a small spring in my step. "I've always wanted a Buddha."

"Let's buy one then," he said.

The stall was empty of anyone to help, so we spent a while browsing the artefacts on the table. "Which one do you want?"

I pouted. "None of them. I don't like them."

"I thought you said…"

"I don't like these, I like the chubby ones." The table was filled with Indian Buddha's but I wanted a Chinese one. "Come on, let's go," I said.

Without knowing why, and in the true style of an *olde-curiosity shop* mystery, Jake stretched his long arms to the back of the table, to an old copper pot, where he dug his hand in and pulled out something wrapped in a piece of dirty cloth. When he opened it up, inside was a little chubby brass Buddha.

I gasped. "That's the one! That's the one I wanted."

"We'll buy it then."

"It looks expensive."

"We can ask someone."

A man came up behind us and sat on a chair next to the stall. I held out the little statue. "Can you tell me how much this is?"

He smiled. "How much is it worth to you?"

No one had ever asked me that before. I certainly couldn't answer such a question. I held the little Buddha in the palm of my hand while I leaned onto my walking stick. I was getting tired. "Why don't you tell us the price and we'll decide if we can afford it?"

He shrugged. "About two hundred." *Two hundred pounds!* We couldn't pay that, even though I told myself I would have given anything to have it. "But you can have it for nothing," he finished.

"What? You can't do that." Jake and I were looking at him as if he'd lost his mind.

The man shook his head. "I picked it up in a little shop in Beijing. I've had it for years but no one ever wanted it. You look as if you need it more than me."

My eyes welled up with unshed tears as I stroked the little Buddha's rounded belly. "You're very kind, but we must pay you."

He shrugged. "Give me a tenner then and take it." We gave him twenty.

When we were walking out of the grand house to go home, I saw the man in an outside cafe talking to three other men who were probably dealers too. They were all laughing at him and I got the impression he was relating the tale of how he gave away the little Buddha to someone who probably would have bought it anyway. As I walked past, he turned his head and smiled at me and I clutched that little Buddha in my hand as if it was a gift from heaven itself.

By the end of the day I was feeling happy again, happy with my little Buddha and the occasion that brought him into my life. "Jake, do you think it's a sign?" I asked.

"Maybe. I'm just glad you're happy."

When he came towards me with a bottle of Brasso and a yellow duster, I grabbed the little Buddha and turned away from the offending rag. "I don't want to clean him!"

"Why not?"

"I don't want to clean the faith off."

NO MEANS YES

Jake when we met.

1999 Just before
my accident

2001 My 40th birthday
(Above with Pauline)

NO MEANS YES

2001 Wheelchair bound.

2002 Wearing a 'practice leg' on holiday in France.

Jake's side of the family.

Chapter 14

-Double or Quits-

A MONTH LATER we were back on track, raring to go for the second course of treatment. The doctors asked us how we felt about not conceiving the first time. To me it didn't matter. That part was over! Round two was going to be the one that would give us our baby. *I was sure of it.*

We began the treatment with the usual blood tests to establish my FSH level and we were given the fertility drugs needed to get the ball rolling. Our own doctor was on holiday. "Don't start the drugs until you hear from us about your FSH level," the duty doctor said. "We'll let you know by the end of the day whether you should start or not."

We knew what we were doing from the first round, so all we needed was our faith that the second course was going to be the one. We waited for the call to tell us to go ahead *or not* but the call never came.

I rang the clinic and left several messages but no one got back to me. When I rang the final time, I got the answer phone. They'd left us high and dry!

Our desperation was not unfounded. We had to take the first injection that evening to stay on track with the IVF cycle, so if we didn't do the injection that night, we'd have to wait another month and I wasn't prepared to put my life on hold for what seemed like poor communication on their part.

At 7.00pm we decided to take the initiative. We agreed that we would take the first injection in order to stay on schedule and then speak to the clinic the next day to find out if we should continue or not. I was still optimistic, nothing could shake it but just after Jake gave me the first injection the phone rang. "It's not a good time to start," the voice at the other end said. "The results have shown your FSH level is too high."

The prognosis had been based on my FSH level being ten and that I had a cyst on my ovary. It didn't add up and I told her so. "I've always had a cyst on my ovary and it hasn't bothered anyone before. In fact, I was told it was quite normal and that a majority of women have them. Why is it an issue now?" I asked.

"A cyst can alter the FSH reading, which distorts the results. The doctor has left instructions that if the reading was over twelve, you shouldn't start."

"But the reading is ten. It's below his cut-off point." I felt a spark of optimism.

"That is where the cyst comes in," she said, "The reading is probably inaccurate."

Huh? It didn't make sense, but she was getting impatient. This woman had taken instructions and no amount of coaxing was going to reverse that decision. "I want to speak to my doctor."

"He's on holiday for another week. We can't contact him. My advice would be to stop the treatment." She must have thought she was negotiating with a crazy woman. "Really, you won't get a positive result based on our numbers."

Numbers! They were talking about science. I was talking about faith. I mean the faith I had that the spirits of my deceased relatives were guiding me along the right path, my mother, and my brother and Jake's brother, John.

-Steve and Johnny-

Six years before, while was were living in the North, one morning, Jake took a call from his daughter, Lorna. His brother had been shot in the head while working in his garage. Everyone was sure he'd been murdered, since he left no suicide note nor had any obvious reason to kill himself. Not only that, the gun used to kill him was found upright against the car he was found leaning against, so there was no way he could have shot himself and left the gun like that.

The police said different. The inquest ruled he had taken his own life, despite how absurd that looked. It was an injustice Jake's mother never recovered from. She'd lost her son and his killer was still out there.

Ironically, one month later, I also had a call. My brother, Steve, had been diagnosed with a malignant brain tumour. In the same year, he died two months after John.

Jake and I have always talked about the irony of us losing our brothers to such tragic circumstances and only months apart. It has never made any sense to us and even now we have no theory about that spiritual aspect. We just use the memory of them and *where* they are to guide us through our future lives.

The nurse on the phone was seriously vexed by my argument. "We've given you our opinion. I can only assure you we know what we're talking about. Please, listen to our advice and suspend the treatment."

That night I couldn't sleep, so I got up and turned on my computer and googled 'FSH'. I discovered that ten was a good FSH number and cysts were normal, confirming my doubts about their prognosis. All night I chewed things over and over in my mind until I exhausted myself and fell asleep. At seven the next morning, Jake brought me a cup of coffee. "Are you okay?"

I held my breath. He was kneeling at the side of the sofa where I'd spent the night. "Jake, don't ask me how I know this but I am absolutely one-hundred percent sure we are supposed to have our baby on this course. I am so sure, I'd bet my life on it. I can't explain how I know it. I just do."

I waited for him to call me crazy, to say it was my hormones and that I was speaking out of desperation, but he didn't say any of that. He simply nodded and said, "Okay."

"What do you mean?"

"I mean, I believe you. I trust your instincts."

I hugged him. "Thank you." Jake had come up trumps for me and I couldn't have loved him more. "What are we going to do?"

He shrugged. "We'll carry on with the treatment. It's our money. If we want to use the drugs, we will."

We figured we would lose a couple of hundred pounds in used drugs if our doctor told us to stop. But, if he opposed the other doctor's decision, then we would be on track with the injections and ready to continue with the treatment. It was a gamble but I told myself everything about IVF was a gamble. The money was the last thing we should be worrying about.

I spoke to the nurse at the clinic and told her our doubts. "We are going to carry on with the injections until we can speak to our own doctor," I said.

We carried on with the daily dose all that week and on Friday I spent another anxious day trying to pin him down. They told me he was in meetings all day but he would ring me back as soon as he was free.

We waited, but he never rang.

-Parenting Paranoia-

I was beginning to get paranoid. Perhaps the meeting was about me and Jake and how they intended to deal with a couple who had openly and shockingly defied the advice of the experts. On the other hand maybe he would ring to say, 'You've passed the test. You did the right thing by taking matters into your own hands.'

At 4.00pm I rang again. He'd gone home.

I spoke to the nurse and she apologised for him not returning my calls and that he would probably ring us in the morning. "But we're going away for the weekend," I said.

"He'll leave you a message if he can't reach you.

We returned on Sunday night after we'd spent the weekend injecting drugs under the cover of darkness.

When we walked through the door, optimistic about life, we both stalled when we saw the answerphone light twitching erratically.

Our doctor had left three messages. 'I need to speak to you. Ring me back.' I pressed the arrow. 'Please get in touch. It's important. You must not carry on with the treatment. Ring me back.' Message number three. 'I cannot stress enough. You must not carry on with the drugs.'

I looked at Jake who was surely wondering how we'd gotten ourselves into such a predicament. We were clearly nuts! "What do we do now?" he said.

"We could always say we didn't get his messages." I started to work it all out in my devious mind. "We're scheduled to go in for a scan tomorrow. We could keep the appointment and say we didn't know we were supposed to stop."

"Right," he said but I could tell he was beginning to lose his confidence. As for me, I had no reservations. I just didn't care what they thought.

That afternoon and again in the evening, as Jake injected me with hormones, I told him to double up the dose.

"Can we do that? Are you sure?"

"What have we got to lose?"

After we whacked them in, by the next morning my confidence was waning. I was about to make a complete fool of myself and would probably get barred from every fertility clinic in the country. Word would get around and in huddled groups the staff would whisper about what fools we were to go against the doctor's orders. I could see them laughing in their tea.

That morning we sat in the waiting room, like two naughty children waiting to see the headmaster. People were staring. *They must all know*, I thought. As the hour moved along, we kept getting overlooked as other patient's names were being called out. People who were turning up later were going in before us. We were surely going to get expelled!

Finally the nurse came out and spoke to us. "Why are you here? We don't need to do a scan if you've stopped the drugs."

"We didn't know what to do, so we kept going with them." My voice was shaking. "We wanted to speak to the doctor first, so we thought we'd keep the appointment for the scan…just to see where we are with things."

She hurried off and brought the doctor back with her. "I left you several messages," he chided.

"We didn't get them."

I could feel Jake fidgeting on his seat next to me as I made my lame excuses. He remained quiet throughout, preferring to leave the deception to me.

The doctor turned to the nurse. "Do a scan."

-Favourite Follicles-

I was shaking with anticipation when we followed the nurse into the scanning room and I watched her expression as she viewed the screen, looking for a sign that would give me the answer I'd been waiting for. She was nodding with her eyes darting back and forth to the screen, writing things down on a chart.

She left the room and brought back the doctor. "You have five follicles" he said. "We normally prefer six, but it's a good result. You can carry on with the treatment."

I can't explain how I felt. I was just happy and relieved. My instinct to carry on with the drugs had been right and now I knew we were going all the way.

During the process of injecting hormone stimulating drugs into my body, I was expecting violent mood swings. It was the part Jake had been dreading. When it didn't happen, we were both surprised and Jake was relieved. I was perfectly happy and content through the whole thing, until Sunday, the final day of injections.

I had picked up an old photo album of my relatives, long dead. Pictures of my beloved mother and my brother, Steve, and all my grandparents; Winnie and Sam and May and Lloyd, and all my deceased aunties and uncles and friends. At the eleventh hour I cried my heart out.

"Hormones!" Jake said.

By the time we got to surgery to withdraw the eggs, the surgeon told us we only had a fifteen percent chance of them being viable. "That's great," I said.

"No, you don't understand," he responded. "That means you have an 85% chance of failing."

"Thanks, but I prefer to look at it as having fifteen percent of making it. Better to be positive."

On Monday morning I was admitted for treatment and when the process was over, the doctor told us that they had managed to get six eggs and that they were pleased. We were elated. As far as I was concerned it only took one.

The next morning the phone rang. It was Steve the embryologist. "Great news," he said "two eggs have fertilised."

"How can this be happening?" I said to Jake. "They said we should stop. What if we had? What if we had stopped?"

"We've still got a long way to go. Don't get your hopes up."

I thanked anyone who was up there listening and guiding us, thanking them for the chance we'd been given, for the miracle of medical science, and for the two little embryos waiting for us in a lab in Manchester.

We were told to go back the next day for the embryo transfer.

In theatre, as I sat on a table with Jake at my side, a TV monitor flickered in front of us. Suddenly, we saw two round black images side by side. There they were, the embryos; our babies. They looked alive, moving. They had divided themselves into several cells, the beginning of their little lives; of all our lives! It was a miracle and as far as I am concerned now, *only* God could have done that.

Fourteen days later, I woke up early. My heart was racing as I waited for the blue line to appear and when it did, I literally couldn't believe what I was seeing.

Against all odds, I was pregnant.

Chapter 15

-Growing Four Legs-

NINE MONTHS LATER I gave birth to twins, one boy and one girl. Together they weighed 15lb 4oz and they were perfect in every way. We named them Tom and Charlotte and from the day they were born, they became *everything*.

After a week, I posted a thank you card and a picture to the clinic for their wall of fame. In the early stages they'd told us that success stories offered people hope, so they always asked for photos of new-borns resulting from successful IVF treatment. When I slipped a photo of Jake and I cradling each of our babies. I couldn't help wondering what would go through their minds when it arrived. I was sure they'd be happy for us but could they also have wondered where they went wrong? Maybe we'll be a case study one day, I thought, as I stuck a stamp on the envelope and posted it off.

Considering my age of forty-two then, some people must have thought I'd have a rough time of my pregnancy, but it couldn't have been more perfect. I had no morning sickness, no stomach pains, no aching back or stretch marks and I carried the babies to the very end. At full term, I was 57inches around the waist, *huge*, but I glowed. My skin was unblemished, my hair was shiny and vibrant and for once I had strong, long healthy nails. The only downside was one of my teeth falling out and that I craved water. I drank gallons of it but it still was never enough. I would have committed murder for a bottle of ice cold water. It was *that* bad.

On my first scan, we discovered there were two babies, and on the second we found out they were a boy and a girl but I already knew that after having two striking dreams, both of them depicting my mother helping me give birth and holding up one blue card and one pink. As far as I was concerned, I didn't need a scan to tell me I was going to give birth to twins; one of each.

When I was just two weeks away from the end of my pregnancy, my old boss, Bill Link, invited us over for a get-together at his house with his family. We often socialised and Jake and I had become very close to him and his wife, Anne. As we left that night, Bill -being Bill- leaned down and kissed my huge stomach twice, one for each baby.

Two weeks later he was dead. He'd had a heart attack and died a few hours later. I mourned him so much, everyone was afraid I'd go into labour early. He'd been such a big influence on my life and losing him was like losing my own father.

The day of his funeral I was huge. I couldn't walk and my face was puffy. Everyone tried telling me not to go but I went for Bill, to say goodbye. The church was bulging with people from his life, in work and in play. He was one of Liverpool's finest, a huge loss to his family and friends who crowded into the church in their hundreds. He had the respect of all and if there was anyone who wasn't there that day, in Bill's immortal words, 'they weren't worth a carrot.'

-Due Dates-

Jake had everything worked out pending the arrival of the babies. At a meeting with the consultant, the doctor said, 'we can pencil in a date for the caesarean around the second week of April.' I saw Jake's eyes light up. He leaned forward in his chair and glanced at the doctor's schedule pinned to the wall. "How about the 14th?" he said. "That's my daughter's birthday."

The doctor laughed as he scoured the planner. "Well, yes, we can do that. I'm free on the fourteenth."

I slumped in the chair waiting for confirmation of my due date, feigning a looking of irritation for been shoved out of the equation but I didn't really mind. Inside I smiled as Jake had his wish; his three children born on the same day, 'triplets' nearly thirty years apart.

When I was just a few months pregnant Jake and I decided to finally get married. We had put it off for as long as we could, because we didn't want to add any more pressure to our already stressful lives but now that the babies were coming, we both felt it was the right time.

The type of ceremony no longer mattered to us. We needed nothing more than the experiences we'd shared together over the past two years to prove our love for one another. Since I was already visibly pregnant, I told Jake I didn't want to walk down the aisle. He agreed. We both wanted to just get it over with and if we could have settled the matter over the phone, we would have.

We sealed the deal with an intimate ceremony in the candlelit library of Nunsmere Hall, a beautiful country house in Cheshire and we spent our honeymoon at home, in the only way we knew how, watching movies in bed while munching chocolates. *Best honeymoon ever!*

We'd already done the whole 'foreign holiday' thing, only six months before. We'd booked a hillside villa overlooking the sea near St. Tropez, just for the two of us. I was still learning to walk properly with my very first artificial leg. They called it a practice leg and it was the most uncomfortable contraption anyone would have the misfortune to wear. It was held on by a strap, which went over the shoulder and around the body and when I sat down, I had to press a button to bend the knee. Sometimes I forgot, so when I took a seat, the leg stuck out in front of me like a ramrod. The worst thing was when I did sit down, the top moved, so when I stood up again, my foot would be pointing out to the side. That meant everywhere I went I was forever altering its position, a constant source of embarrassment and discomfort.

The idea of the villa was being able to lock ourselves away for a fortnight and enjoy the sunshine, swimming, reading and eating. Of course we also wanted to explore the area, so we went off for a couple of days taking in the sights. One day we came to a little village holding a street market. It was laid out on a hill and we parked at the top. When I got out of the car and turned my leg to point in the right direction, I looked at the acutely declining slope and I stopped. "Jake, I can't do it. I can't do that hill."

"Yes, you can," he said. "We'll take it slow and I'll hold your hand."

He was clearly mad! I was shaking my head. "And how will I get back up? No! Can't do it! It's impossible."

He looked exasperated with me but it must have been thirty-eight degrees in the shade and I was more than aware of what my stupid leg was capable of, or more to the point, *not* capable of!

"Can you see that?" He pointed to a canopied stall with long, coloured linen dresses hanging from its sides.

I spotted a slim fitting long mauve dress with embroidery along the top and bottom. "Ooh, I like that."

"I'll buy it for you. But you have to go down and get it."

I began to feel more motivated. "If I get stuck down there, you can carry me back up," I shouted as I slowly made the descent.

Suffice to say I made it and true to his word he bought me the dress. When I got it home it didn't fit. *That figured!*

I've always felt God picked the wrong person to cope with wearing an artificial leg. I have never been the right shape or size to get on with it. Since I'm not exactly svelte, or physically fit and I have big feet and I'm tall, with a lot further to fall than other amputees, I often wondered why it had to me.

As for falling, I did that a lot. My first was when I was still in hospital and the nurse got me out of bed for the first time. My brain still hadn't registered I only had one leg, so as soon as I stood up, I fell over.

The second time was in the gym on my very first attempt at walking with a decent prosthesis and a mechanical knee. The idea was to push the leg with the muscles in the hip and thigh and put weight into the toe to unlock the knee. It was a technique I needed to master before I took it out for a spin but as I moved the first step, the knee was too loose and didn't lock, so down I went. I didn't hurt myself but that single fall knocked a lot of my confidence and it took me years to stop worrying about falling every time I walked.

When I was pregnant I had to stop wearing the prosthesis as I got closer to full term. My bump was huge, so it was no surprise when the babies arrived on the 14th April 2003, they were 15lb collectively.

They were perfect in very way. Tom arrived first, kicking and screaming followed two minutes later by Charlotte, who opened her eyes and had a good look round. Jake was the first to hold them and my dad sneaked into the delivery suite when he shouldn't have been in there.

We'd made it. Now all we had to do was raise them without killing them.

Chapter 16

-Searching for God-

I HAD EVERYTHING READY for the baby's arrival. We'd moved the table out of the kitchen, leaving us with a small area at the end where we put a cot, a nursing chair and a changing table. For the first few months they would sleep together in the day and then at night we'd take them upstairs to our room where the other cot was placed at the end of our bed. *I had it all worked out!*

The day they came home was a wonderful moment, all bundled up in their new white outfits, one with a touch of pink and the other with a touch of blue but despite their angelic and peaceful appearance, it didn't take long for us to discover they were ticking time bombs. It took them only one night to disrupt all our best laid plans and frankly, I didn't think they'd be that way. I thought they'd be more agreeable!

It took us two days to pluck up the courage to bathe them. I'd acquired a plastic baby bath, which I intended to fill up from the downstairs shower and then, with the bath on the floor, I could sit on the loo seat and bathe them. Jake wasn't happy with the idea, saying it was impractical, so, as we started arguing about it, our worst nightmare happened when Tom stopped breathing. Once we regained our faculties, I grabbed Charlotte while Jake picked up Tom and wrapped him in a towel. He tried stimulating his chest, but his eyes remained closed and he was limp and still not breathing. *This can't be happening*, I thought. *We can't lose him now after all we'd been through.* "Jake, get him to the hospital," I shouted. "Leave us here and just go."

Jake rushed to the hall and brought in the car seat. He put Tom inside as I was praying and crying, *don't let him die, please don't let him die.*

Then he woke up. Good as new!

When we relayed the tale to the midwife, she said babies have a complex defence system. Tom had sensed our confusion in the shower and had simply shut himself down. It was one of the most terrifying incidents we'd had as new parents, but it wasn't the only one.

-Visiting Vices-

Within a week of the babies being home, the visitors came by the lorry load. They all wanted to see the twins and our midwife warned us it would happen. She told us we would be better off putting a sign on the door saying '*Mother busy with babies, come back another day*'. Seriously!

Actually, we were pleased that everyone was so keen to see the babies. We would have felt worse if they hadn't have bothered. "Besides," I said "A sign on the door telling everyone to go away would be insulting." I wondered why she didn't know that.

We understood her thinking when the pressure of visitors became unbearable. We didn't just have visitors from our friends in the North, we also had visitors from both our families and they all stayed over. We provided beds, meals and entertainment and our routine with the babies got so messed up, Jake and I were physically and mentally exhausted.

We kept a note book permanently on the kitchen work bench. It was our house rule to log every feed the babies had. Which one of them had been fed, and how many ounces they'd drunk. It was hardly ever the same, because Tom was always more hungry than Charlotte and he couldn't get enough of the stuff. When the visitors came, they all wanted to feed them and our note book was often ignored. We'd put aside an area for stacking, sterilising and preparing bottles with a separate kettle used just for the bottle making process but when the visitors came, suddenly our dedicated spot became a resting-ground for handbags, newspapers and car keys.

When we planned our routine together, Jake agreed he wouldn't walk around with the babies. It was something I couldn't physically do myself, so we didn't want them getting used to being soothed that way. *But* the visitors didn't get that. After everyone ignored my pleas and strolled up and down the kitchen with the babies thrown over their shoulders, when they went home, we were left with two screaming infants who wouldn't stop crying unless they were paraded along the length of the house. *Great!*

As a new mother who was physically disabled, I began to feel vulnerable. Some of the visitors, without any regard for propriety and without asking, took the babies off me when they started to cry. I'm sure they thought they were being helpful but I felt sensitive because of my incapacity and wanting to do everything my body would allow to look after my own babies.

Throughout it all I never complained but I often wished I had. They were my babies, my responsibility but I didn't want to hurt anyone's feelings, or sound paranoid, and I didn't want to be the cause of destroying friendships. Inside, I felt hurt that they weren't sensitive enough to think about how I felt and how their actions made my limitations look so obvious, when my lack of mobility was forever being brought to the fore.

Beyond the chaos, the best part of it all was watching Jake being the most excellent father and my own father being a doting and completely besotted grandfather. To me he was the father I had always wanted him to be, head over heels in love with his grandchildren and one hundred percent supportive of me. Despite all the misery I felt with other people's interference, the love I got from Jake and my father was my biggest joy.

Finally to end a chapter of my life and to begin another, when the twins were over a year old, Jake and I decided to make a fresh start. We were *over* the North of England and even though all our friends were there, we felt it was time to start a new life.

So, in 2004 we emigrated to France.

Chapter 17

-C'est la Vie-

I WAS TOLD EARLY ON in my Christian life to push the devil behind me when I felt he was trying to distract me from God. It's a good way of letting go but I wish I'd known that the first morning in our French home, when we opened the shutters to let the sun in. That was when the devil came in too, sticking to me like glue until I finally quit his destructive evil, left France and turned to God.

La Grande Etouble was an ancient farmhouse comprising of three cottages joined together, sitting amid a five-acre vineyard. It was the French dream, half-habitable while the other side waited to be lovingly restored.

We'd sold our house in England at the peak of the housing boom, leaving us with enough equity to survive for a year and renovate half the house. In our infinite wisdom, the idea was to incorporate a gite at the end cottage to provide us with an income. The rest of the house was habitable, although not decorated to our taste. We thought the large lounge served better as a kitchen, big enough to hold a large dining table, since it was the French (or was it the Italians), who said you should always eat in the same room you cooked in. Doors opened onto the terrace where the sun spent most of the day, and a smaller room extended from the main one, where we situated our massive twin armoires we'd dubbed Louis and Douis. *Don't ask me why!*

With a lick of paint, we decided the old kitchen with its original décor of brown cabinets, brown floor tiles and brown teapot-print wallpaper, could be turned into a good sized salon since the fireplace was big enough to sit inside.

Behind that, a smaller room housed the ancient boiler; one of those contraptions you could imagine starting-up by banging on the sides with a hammer. We discovered that wasn't far from the truth when we had to send for the previous owner to explain the phone system he had installed himself as a DIY project.

Monsieur Viot arrived armed with big a tool box. He spoke no English and as far as we were aware he didn't once mention the word telephone- not in any language! He did manage to mutter something however, when he walked straight past us to the boiler room at the back of the house. There he dismantled, turned and cogged, spat and wrenched, bleeded and watered the monstrous machine, for half-an-hour, before he closed his tool box and got up to leave. Just as I was about to stop him mid-exit to explain that foreign word which had clearly stumped him: *Telephone!* Jake suddenly came crashing through the door.

I forgot all miscommunication with M. Viot when I saw our two-and-half-year old terrible twins hanging from Jake's strong grasp, covered from head to toe in white gloss paint and laughing as if they'd just struck Christmas.

Clutching his tool box, Monsieur Viot made a hasty retreat, as Jake ran up the stairs and threw our bluer-than-white kids in the bath, where the paint, thankfully, came off in one soaking.

It took another month before we finally got the phones fixed!

-Troublé a doublé-

People joke about *double-trouble* but if they haven't had twins, they really have no idea. Ours were *very* active and they developed quickly with a keen sense of what was going on around them. Alarmingly so!

One of their favourite parent-wind-ups was to run away at every opportunity, which was great fun for them when mummy and daddy came chasing after them, but for me, it was the worst characteristic they could have possessed. Even now I ask myself why it had to be that one. If they'd had a habit of throwing tantrums in the supermarket, I could have dealt with that, but the running away thing…that was my worst nightmare!

At the start of our new adventure, we'd booked a cabin on the ferry, simply to serve as a giant playpen. The idea was for Jake to get some sleep since he would be driving through the night, and for me to rest while the kids played and ran about like the little mad people they were. But, as Jake snored in the opposite bunk and when I closed my eyes for a critical blinking second, the two of them unlocked the door and escaped into the ferry wilderness.

By the time I reached the entrance, as if it had been planned, they had split up, with the foresight to know their enjoyment would be prolonged if I had to chase one after the other.

Held upright by an artificial leg and a walking stick, I chased them along the many corridors, past numerous closed cabin doors whilst the boat rocked over the waves of the English Channel.

I caught Charlotte first and threw her back into the room where Jake still slept. And after threatening her with all sorts of horrible things, I went back into the fray to find Tom.

I was beginning to lose all my strength by the time I found him sprinting along a corridor, but like all mums who have untold energy when it comes to their kids, I kept on going. After I saw him heading for a glass door leading out to the deck and the rough black sea beyond, I prayed for the second time since becoming a parent, when a picture came into my mind of him going over the side and perishing in the freezing water. That's when I switched to survival mode and stopped running. "Mummy's got some chocolate buttons," I called.

That was all it took. He turned about and with a gleeful chuckle he came running back towards me allowing me to grab him and never let go. As half of me cursed, the other half squeezed him tight and thanked *someone* for stopping him falling into the sea. Was it God or was it chocolate? Maybe it was a bit of both!

-L'arrivée-

Jake drove through the night for six hours while the rest of us slept. When we woke up, we were in South-West France, near Bordeaux, in a little town called St Ciers de Cannesse.

Our newly purchased residence was surrounded on all sides by grapevines. It was December, so the place didn't look as good as it had in the summer when we agreed to buy it. The vines were only twigs sticking out of the ground, compared to their summer bloom, when they flourished with budding juicy black grapes.

At noon, we headed into the centre of Bordeaux and parked a short distance from the notaire's office. The twins were getting agitated considering how long they'd been confined to their car seats, and we were all hungry and tired. It took hours to go through the documents, but by the end, after the kids had driven us insane with their demands, we would have signed our life away just to get out of there.

It was night by the time we got back to the house. Outside, a devilish storm was brewing. The kids were screaming with frustration and I was in terrible pain after wearing my leg for so long. Jake was all done in and we were all grubby from the events of the day.

"I'll go and sort the bed out," Jake said as I shoved another warm bottle of milk into the hungry mouths of my children.

Outside, the storm was firing on all cylinders. Then the lights went out. Our first power cut! The thunder was so powerful it rocked the eaves and white lightning squeezed its fingers between the cracks in the shutters.

When Jake came back downstairs, we lit the only candle we could find, and gathered up the children now clean after being washed with a wet flannel and dressed in their pink and blue pyjamas. Up the stairs we climbed, bearing our heavy loads.

I was ready to drop by the time we reached the top, but as we walked along the boarded landing, squeaking beneath our feet, Jake pushed open the door leading to our room. When the candlelight revealed our beautiful antique French bed assembled and dressed with brand new crisp white sheets, I sighed with anticipation, feeling enormous appreciation of a husband who knew how to make me happy.

Nothing was said. The four of us simply climbed under the duvet smelling of fresh linen, and within seconds, while the storm raged outside, exhausted, we slept.

Chapter 18

-Storms of Sunshine-

WE AWOKE THAT FIRST MORNING to the sun streaming through the open windows, even though it was just a week before Christmas. We secured the children with reins as we explored the grounds, going from the house to our own little woodland and up again to the orchard with various trees of apple, pear, plum, chestnut with a very large fig tree in the corner shading a perfect lawn. Beyond the garden was our four acre vineyard, beckoning our children to run and hide.

"We need a fence," I said. "If they get into the vines, we may never find them again." The vines in the Gironde area were not normally fenced from the property owner's gardens, but we knew we'd have no peace if we didn't imprison our two children, *like Colditz.*

According to my mother-in-law, their escape gene must have come from Jake's side of the family, since at the age of three, when she took him to the beach, to stop him from running off she had to tie him with a length of rope to the leg of the deckchair. I knew it had to be Jake's fault our twins acted like detainees!

That first day in our new French farmhouse, outside on the terrace, we feasted on soup and fresh bread. It was a dismal dark brown colour (the terrace – not the soup!) so it became our goal to get rid of it and replace it with something more cheerful. As we munched on *Heinz*, since we still didn't know where to find a shop, we looked back at the house where the old Gironde stone walls were black with grime and the dark green shutters that made the whole concept so unattractive. When a car zoomed past the gateless entrance and tooted its horn, we waved back. We knew everyone in the village would now know *the English* had arrived, since no sensible French man would dine outdoors in the middle of winter.

After Christmas, Jake went back home to bring back more of our things. We still hadn't sold our house in England and until we did, money was going to be short. The day he left I got nervous. Being in a strange country was one thing, but being *alone* in a strange country was something else.

The children were no wiser to normal safety requirements, but I was optimistic they were heading for their second birthday and starting school in September, and that their maniac behaviour would surely diminish the older they got.

When Jake left for his trip back to England, the twins must have spent many a night under the cover of darkness, conspiring how to break free from their overprotective mother. Together, with their own way of communicating, they worked out how to turn a key and how to push down on the heavy lever handles, so that when I went into the kitchen and saw the door wide open, I knew I was in trouble.

Jake had put up a temporary mesh gate on the open entrance to the driveway, but when I rushed outside to find them, I saw it had been pulled away from its fasteners and now it was lolling and flapping in the breeze. The gateway opened onto the road running past the house, where the occasional car speeded along at a rate of kilo-knots. When I stepped onto the tarmac and looked up and down, I couldn't see them. They were gone.

-Chocolate Promises-

I had to stop myself from crying when I called their names with every octave I could muster. A car came towards me, so I waved frantically, hoping the occupant would stop and help, but he sped past, staring at me out the window as if I'd lost my mind.

In the valley I saw a flash of colour. *Pink and Blue.*

They were on Monsieur Raymond's land, outside his house centred within a vast vineyard. It was starting to rain. "Tom and Charlotte," I called. I saw them laugh as one after the other, they charged into a barn at the side of Chez Raymond.

I ran, but I use the word sparingly since I couldn't exactly *run* on my artificial leg, but as I used my stick as a third leg, I went speed-walking along our neighbour's private road, charging like a bull after her pink and blue bullocks.

When I reached the end, a black dog sprang out from around the corner of the house. He stood in front of the barn doors, barking and snarling, daring me to go past him. But I did dare! As I moved to the side of him, he pounced on me, unaware the leg I'd stuck out for him to bite was made of metal and covered in foam.

I felt no pain when he grabbed me with his snarling teeth and held on. He must have been wondering when he was going to taste blood, as I leaned on my free leg (the real one) to glance around the doors to see inside. I forgot the dog chewing on metal, when I saw the whole barn filled with saws and cutting tools hanging from the ceiling and every wall. It looked like a military stash and there amongst it all were my two-year olds having the best of times.

It must have been the terror-stricken tone to my voice, which made them come out and take my hand. Behind me, the dog was being pulled off my leg by an old woman dressed from head to toe in black. She was saying something about how cute the kids were. *Seriously!?*

I held my stick horizontally while I clutched them both and marched them back down the drive towards home. I limped, holding myself up with every muscle I could clench. I couldn't speak. I was ready to drop from exhaustion. Out of breath and on the verge of tears, I got them to the back door, and as I let go of Charlotte's hand to push the handle down, she took off again, out through the temporary gate and back to the vineyard of Monsieur Raymond.

I shook my head and screamed after her. "CHARLOTTE!!!" But she was gone once more.

I shouted at Tom to stay in the house and locked him in. He was alone in the kitchen and I could hear him crying as I once more took off in search of my daughter. I was in serious pain from the pressure of my leg as I crossed the road, but I couldn't stop. I saw her, a blonde vision dressed in pink, charging up the aisle between the vines. I don't know how I got up the grass bank, but I did, and as the rain came down I went after her, hobbling along deep muddy tracks hoping and praying she would stop.

Up ahead, at the end of the aisle, I saw a car pass by. My child was heading for the main road and she was laughing like she didn't have a care in the world.

"Charlotte," I called, faking a lack of desperation she'd probably want to exploit. "I've got chocolate." But she kept running. I must have tried that before and failed to deliver and she'd remembered! "Charlotte, do you want some chocolate. Yum yum, come back before I finish it all."

She stopped only a couple of metres from the road, where she turned and ran back towards me and into my arms.

I had nothing left to give. I put her inside the kitchen, locked the door and I sat at the table and cried.

When I felt little fingers in my hair, I looked up to see Tom sucking on a dummy looking as if he was about to go asleep and Charlotte, sucking her thumb, stroking my face and wondering why I was crying.

-Talking & Walking-

I like to think of the times I had with my kids when they were younger as a series of blips. When I look back at the events that happened almost on a daily basis, I always shake my head at the memory of their crazy antics.

After we'd put them to bed one summer night, we waited a while for them to fall asleep, before Jake and I, with a glass of wine in hand, went out back to the covered stone terrace. We'd often spend evenings out there, even when summer storms raged over rolling hills of vines in the distance. It was one of our favourite spots.

That particular night there was no storm, only a cooling breeze wafting from the north, making us sigh with sleepy contentment. We spent the evening talking about the kids and our life in France and our plans for the house and how we were going to make a living in that foreign land, and afterwards, when we went upstairs to bed and we looked in to check on the kids, we both stopped as if time had stood still.

There was Tom and Charlotte lying flat out on the floor in exhausted sleep in what resembled some sort of crime scene (*Picture included*). We had to wonder at their mentality when we saw the carnage. What normal children would have thought of dismantling two cots so they could use them to make ladders to climb over the gate on the entrance of the bedroom door? And knowing they needed to get back in without being discovered, to take every piece of clothing from our room to make a mountain to climb up and get back over? No safety gear required! The fact they did it without being heard was impressive even by their standards, like pussycat burglars on a rampage.

The following day we fitted a baby monitor they couldn't bury under a pillow, and doubled up on the gates, one on top of the other. Caught and imprisoned. *For life!*

-Fanciful Freedom-

When we found a lake not far from our house, we thought we'd discovered the perfect place to hang out. France had many manmade lakes, inland, all free to use, with little beaches to frolic on and trees to shade beneath.

It was at this idyllic location we took a picnic to allow the kids to play on the beach whilst Jake and I relaxed. We enjoyed watching them paddling in the shallow water and making sand castles with their new bucket and spade, but the blip occurred when Jake closed his eyes at the same time as me. We were only soaking up the rays, confident our children were happy playing on the sand in front of us, but when I opened my eyes, the kids were gone.

"Where are they?" I screamed as Jake shot into an upright position.

My vision stretched to the other side of the lake, where I could just make out two small people running in the water towards the next island. We knew the water was shallow, but we didn't know that shallowness extended that far.

They were laughing when Jake waded over to get them back and when I stretched my neck and shaded my eyes from the blinding sun, I watched as he grabbed Tom in one hand and Charlotte in the other, and dragged them back to shore. *(Picture included)*

-The Great Escape-

Another blip occurred when we were washing dishes two rooms away from the kid's twenty-foot long playroom. We'd sacrificed the space to allow them theirs, since their lack of freedom at the age of three seemed to be an issue. "They've gone quiet." Jake said.

We stared into each other's eyes as we realised we hadn't heard them for over ten minutes. We knew all the doors were locked and that the keys hung well out of reach, but still... We rushed to the playroom. *They'd be fine. We were sure.*

When we saw a stack of chairs wobbling precariously next to the open door leading to the back terrace, we knew we were in trouble. They'd made a climbing frame to reach the keys that had once hung from a beam overhead. Now the keys were gone and so were they.

Beyond the terrace, another gate hung listlessly ajar, leading to acres of vines running in bushy rows, packed with black grapes.

Jake ran off to the end of a tier and searched each row. I took the other side, limping on my leg, my only prop, since I hadn't had time, nor the inclination, to go back to get my stick.

I was exhausted and panting for breath, speed walking everywhere. Then, as I stood in the middle of the road searching the horizon, a car came towards me with its headlights flashing. Inside Tom and Charlotte were waving at funny mummy looking as if she was going to fall over and die.

With bare feet and wearing just their pyjamas, they had raced through the vines, up to the road at the top of the hill, crossed over without getting splattered by a passing car, and into our neighbour's hotel on the far corner. From her window, Helene had seen them standing next to her swimming pool, ready to jump in and swim, or drown. "Ou est maman?" she'd asked.

They pointed in the direction of home. "La maison," they squealed.

When they were finally returned, we took them back into the house, washed their feet, and put them to bed. Blip over!

Chapter 19

-A Chat at the Chateau-

THE LONG SUMMERS STARTED in April and ended in October, offering us glorious weather as every meal was eaten outdoors, feasting on daily fresh bread, and red wine from our own vineyard. For the onlookers it was tranquil, but the reality held no such romantic charm.

Jake gave up trying to speak French very early on. That left me to take on the task, and a task it was. I spent every waking hour trying to learn the language, buying every bit of software I could find and playing cassettes in the car when I would have much preferred music. I attempted to become engaged in conversations with all the French people we met and when everyone had gone to bed, I practised grammar, trying everything I could to master the verbs and the gender of each word. It took me six months before I could be confident enough to have a conversation with a native, but I never really enjoyed it since my French was never that effective. The worst part for me was trying to understand what the French were saying. If they spoke too fast, I missed the words that translated into the crux of the story.

A week after we'd moved in, Jake and I were invited to dinner up at the chateau which leased our vines and made our wine: *Chateau Mercier*. Philippe and Martina Chety were the force behind the very lucrative business and along with their son and heir, Christophe, and daughter, Isabelle, they welcomed Jake and I into their fold as if we were part of the family.

That evening we deposited the children with a babysitter, wished her good luck, and arrived at the chateau promptly at seven. We were told much later that the French *never* turned up on time and that to be half-an-hour late was considered the norm. I couldn't cope with that custom at all, since I'd been a stickler for keeping good time all my life, so we arrived on the dot. None of the people at the dinner party spoke English except for Isabelle, who proficiently translated our discussions in her charming French way.

When the first course of oysters was served, we excused ourselves from accepting their offer of *servez-vous*. They tried to coax us and even though Jake refused point blank, I tried one for the sake of propriety. To me it tasted of sea water and nothing else.

The oysters were served with a delicious white wine until the next course came and all our glasses were emptied into a silver bucket. The second course was sausages. Long, very savoury sausages, which Jake, once again, refused to eat. When I kicked him in the shin and he rubbed his leg under the table, I whispered "Just eat one and suffer." He grimaced as he took one of the sausages and placed it on his plate. "Eat half and then hide the rest under the salad," I said.

When the sausages were gone, the family were happily inebriated and getting lively by the minute. Jake only had one glass of red, since he was driving. As for me, I knew I had to get out of there walking on an artificial leg, so I drank in moderation. The silver bucket was useful for ditching the wine we didn't drink, and by the third course I doubt they even noticed.

Jake was overjoyed when they announced the next course as steak, until an array of raw red meat was brought out on a large platter. *Surely not!*

We were relieved when Martina threw them onto a metal rack above the open fire in the hearth. "I've never seen that done before," I remarked to Isabelle.

She pouted as she considered my question. "Yes, we cook like this in the winter. Why not?" She had a point. The fire was an effective indoor barbecue.

When the steaks were removed after only seconds of cooking time, Jake started to look pale. He liked his steaks well-done, so it was no surprise when he held up his hand to refuse.

"You don't like steak?" Isabelle said as she speared one of the practically raw rumps and released it onto her plate.

"He likes it *Bien Cuit*," I said, rolling my eyes.

"*Maman,*" Isabelle shouted, "Put the steak back on the fire."

Martina laughed and nodded her head "*Ah, oui, oui.* The Engleesh…they like steak black, *non?*"

"*Oui, Oui,*" said Jake.

I just wanted to throttle him.

By the time an array of French cheese was served, Jake was on fine form. "Any cheddar?" he said as they all laughed.

-La Rendezvous-

Not mastering the language gave us problems from other quarters. Registering the kids for school was one and dealing with matters that relied on official procedures and red tape. One of them was contacting the French social services to register for prosthetic care. Since we were in the EU, the funds used in England to provide me with an artificial leg, would be transferred to the French state. All I had to do was to go and make sure that happened.

I was requested to attend a meeting in Bordeaux and as Jake stayed outside with the children, I was ushered into a large conference room. Inside was a single chair placed at the back of the room, and in front, six tables were lined-up side by side with twelve French officials sitting behind them. None of them spoke English, so I presented my case using words and phrases I had practiced beforehand –*Une jambe cassée*; *d'amputer*; *J'ai besoin d'une jambe artificielle*; *Payé par les Anglais*...

A few of them smiled, but I got the distinct impression most of them didn't believe I had a false leg, so when they asked to see it, I pulled up my trouser leg and gave them an eye full.

Our next challenge was to register the kids at school in the village. No one spoke English there either so we had to muddle through with the help of a friend.

The school was delighted to enrol some English children. Tom and Charlotte were only five months past their second birthday when they started and they were still having warm milk from bottles, but by the time they reached three, they were bilingual, which was pretty impressive for ones so young.

But the best memory we have of them going to school in France was when they came home and Jake parked up outside the house. That's when they ran across the garden whilst stripping off their clothes, and jumped into our very own swimming pool.

That was something else!

Chapter 20

-Writing for Life-

DESPITE THE TRIALS and *many* tribulations, after two years we finally reached a point of settling into our new habitat, remodelling our home while raising the children. Jake was spending many nights away in his new job as a driver for an international removal firm, the kids were at school most of the time and I was bored.

Then one day when I was cleaning the kitchen floor, God laid His hand on me.

It was hot outside, even though it was still early and I had thrown open the doors to make a breeze waft through the house as perspiration ran from my forehead into my eyes. When I stopped and wiped my hand across my brow, something on the television made me look at the screen. TVam was showing a girl demonstrating some fitness exercises while sitting in a wheelchair. She was an above-knee amputee like me, and she had just written her autobiography; *Just a Step,* by Leanne Grose. Our connection was clear so I went on Amazon and bought her book.

When it arrived two days later, I sat down to read about Leanne's life and the tale she had written of her courage and bravery. She had lost her leg to cancer, and like myself, she wasn't about to let it get in the way of the life she had planned. When I finished her story, I got in touch to congratulate her on her achievement. She graciously sent me an email in response and after we conversed for a while, she encouraged me to write my own story. I mentioned it to Jake. "You know I was saying the other day how I wished I could write a book. How about I try writing my autobiography?"

He shrugged without looking up from his paper. "Give it a go."

I was excited and nervous both at the same time. I knew how to put together a killer complaint letter or a job application, but to write a book! I didn't know where to start. I began when I sat at my computer and pulled up a blank page and within a fortnight I'd written fifteen-thousand words. I thought I'd finished. How many words does it take to fill a normal book? I wondered. So I googled it... An autobiography: maybe 50-60,000! I chewed my lip as I looked at the finished manuscript sitting on the desk next to me. I rang my dad. 'What do I do?'

"Put more pronouns in," he said 'That'll pad it out a bit."

Good idea!

I called it 'Two Shining Lights' and sent it out to several agents in the UK, confident I would be contacted within a week and that the whole saga would probably come down to a bidding war.

My first rejection came after two months and two more followed. I didn't get it. *Why weren't they banging down my door?*

I had one positive response from an agent who said he enjoyed reading about my life, but was it really true?

Huh!

Another told me I didn't stand a chance, not while Jordon was having hers published.

Another wrote back and said he was interested in looking at the manuscript, but his partner had become involved and she'd told him to pull out.

"No one wants it," I cried to Jake. "I'm no good."

The next day he came home with a brand new silver laptop. "Keep trying."

-A Killa Script-

I recall an occasion in my childhood, which must have affected me in ways I'd never thought about before. I was eleven-years old when my teacher gave everyone in my class an assignment to write a story. It was up to us, she told the children, to write whatever we wanted to write about and *how much* we wanted to write.

Me! I wrote a novel.

The story was a whodunit mystery set in a hospital ward where the characters and the lives of the patients and staff moved the plot along. I remember toiling over it day after day, loving the story I'd created because I was able to step inside the scenes and lose myself from the real world.

When I was announced the winner of the task, I was beyond proud. I was asked to go to the front of the class to accept a prize of a printed certificate. As everyone stopped clapping and I faced my peers, the teacher said, "Wendy didn't win because it was the best story in the class, but because she wrote a whole book."

Her comment demoralising me so much, I never wrote again, until over thirty-years later, when in the early hours of the morning I looked at my manuscript and decided to turn it into a novel. If no one was going to believe my story, I thought, I may as well go the fiction route.

With my new shiny silver laptop, I changed my life story into a work of fiction and created a thriller. Suddenly my fingers were travelling over the keyboard as if I had been writing all my life. The prose wasn't perfect, but the substance was there. I had invented a story with a mixed bag of characters, suddenly doing something I never knew I could; write. It was a revelation. It had taken me a lifetime to finally realise I possessed an imagination and the ability to make up story lines in order to pull a whole novel together.

I named the book *In the Shadow of Strangers*, and used my grandmother's maiden name of *Killa* to rename the lead character. Then I sent it out to agents.

Those were the days when kindle and self-publishing hadn't even been heard of so the only route I could take was the traditional one. I even tried to bypass the agents and go straight to the publisher. *Not allowed!*

More rejections came back, except for one energetic up-and-coming literary agent. He asked me to put together a synopsis, to use one page for each chapter, and to get it to him by Monday. *It was Friday!*

It was hot as hell outside, maybe forty degrees. "Jake, I've got to write this stuff by Monday," I said. "I need to lock myself away and need you to look after the kids on your own."

"Give me an hour," he said.

Don't get me wrong about my husband, he's no saint! His flaws are many and I'd be happy to discuss them with you but that weekend he was my saviour when he set up a desk in the summer house overlooking the pool. He put in a lamp, my laptop and a printer and a small fridge filled with water and a bottle of wine. He even set up a little camp bed in the corner for me to rest when I wasn't writing. I spent the next two days putting together the work he had asked me to do and as I typed I listened to my family outside frolicking in the pool. When I finished, I held those one hundred pages in my hand like a lifeline and I kissed the package before I sent it off.

One week later he rejected it.

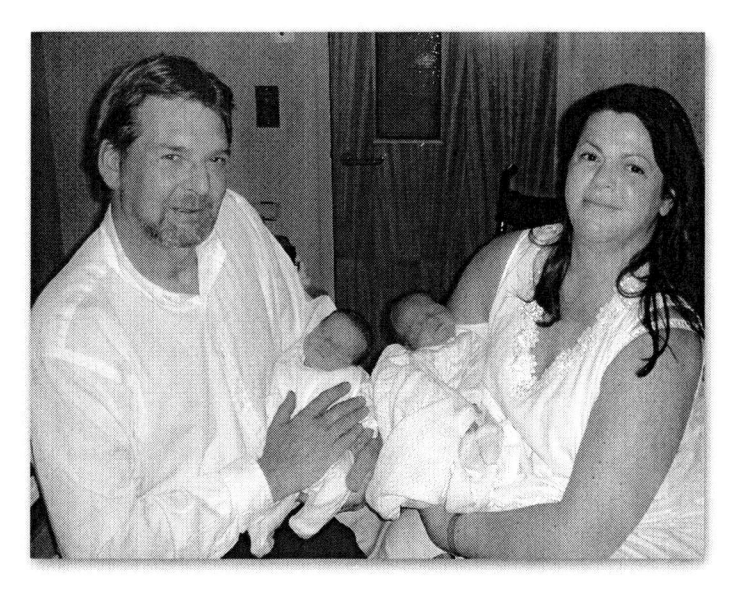

April 2003 One pink, one blue. Perfect!

Getting ready to rumble

An advert for windowlene

2005 Moving to France

WRITING FOR LIFE

The In the Vineyard

First day of school at 2½yr

Dragging them out of the lake.

Crime scene.

another amputee in there, which made me feel pretty unique in a strange sort of way.

I could only surmise what went on back-of-house. My guess was they Google'd *female amputees* and did a scribble on a notepad. They sourced the same leg I already had, called a *total knee*, and I was handed over to one of their senior prothetists, Guy (pronounced *Gee*), who spoke a little English.

The socket is the hardest part to get right on an artificial leg. It has to be a good fit and moulded to your body like a second skin. That was okay in theory, but when you're a pre-menopausal female whose body size fluctuates as many times as she has cereal for breakfast, the whole process gets harder. One day it fits and the next day it doesn't. *C'est la vie!*

The mould is made by covering the top of your leg with Plaster of Paris. They then make a temporary socket made of opaque plastic, which they use to make the fit perfect while you're wearing it. After a week they bring you back for a fitting of the real thing, but then they take it off you again so that they can tidy it all up and attach the knee joint to the pole that acts as a tibia. They attach the foot to the other end of the pole, which invariably looks like a flesh coloured lump of plastic you see on mannequins in a shop window. Then they cover the whole ensemble in foam and pull a skin-coloured stocking over the top. *Voila*. That's your leg.

Mine weighed a stone so it was like lugging around a sack of potatoes. When I sat down I had to get used to sitting on a hard lump of plastic that felt more like a rock covered in sandpaper as the day went on, but the worst part was when you went to someone's house and left a dent on their lovely new wooden toilet seat!

Or you can't get on the floor to play with your kids because your leg sticks out in front of you, making you ill-equipped to manoeuvre properly or worst of all, you can't get up again. You can climb stairs, but you can only do it one step at a time, like a toddler and, of course, swimming is out. You have to take it off to do that, but then there's the problem of actually reaching the pool because you can't walk to it without one on. *Beaucoup de problèmes!*

-La Damn Jambe-

The clinic went through the process of making me a new leg. They seemed pretty excited when they brought me back each week to test their prototype, until finally, *voila*, it was ready for me to take home. The trouble with a total knee, if you don't know the workings of it as well as you know the veins on the back of your hands, you're not going to get it right. So, when my leg man told me to take a step backwards, down I went, crashing into a wheelie table, which didn't serve to break my fall.

It turned out Guy hadn't adjusted the back part of the knee to lock on a backward step, so after I was blamed for a lack of aptitude, I was told to take it home and start practising. After crashing to the hard floor of our kitchen every time I stepped backwards, I finally deduced it had to be returned to the clinic, where after a number of weeks they discovered a bolt they hadn't tightened. *C'est la vie!*

As for the covering…I was dubious when a few weeks previously, he took me out to the garden in front of the clinic and used his phone to take a photograph of my left leg. He even asked me to smile! He then scanned the photo onto a silicone cover, so that it matched my other leg, freckles and all. I thought it was quite ingenious, despite it suiting only my shin, whereas the foot still looked like a lump of orange plastic.

A year later I heard about a young girl in our village who'd had a motorbike accident and had to lose her leg. It seemed ironic that there were now two amputees in the same French village. I wrote to her, offering my love and support, offering her hope with something that seems so devastating in the beginning.

When things weren't working out with the first leg man, I decided to try the clinic she used. He was a one-man band and he operated in a little private gym every Tuesday. The set-up didn't sound as professional as the last lot but I have to say he was one of the best I'd had. He took on board all my issues and he didn't even speak English, but we muddled through perfectly okay in French.

He made me a soft socket with holes cut into it so that when I sat down the flesh of my thighs dispersed evenly. And that was *une très grande réussite*.

Chapter 22

-Angels and Demons-

I OFTEN WONDER where God was when I found myself sinking in that foreign place. Of course I realise now He was right by my side. I just didn't know it *then*.

We all suffer periods in our lives when the devil steps in and destroys our peace of mind, just like a cancer that takes over, growing until its host is destroyed. Despite that, I still felt I was being cared for from above and it was that single notion which carried me through each tumultuous moment as it came, stamping out the devil's raging darkness.

I'm physically broken, *that's true*, however my mental state was always the thing I had control over. But as strong as I was and as hard as I tried in those days to force negativity from my door, there were times when my strength just wasn't enough.

My spirit slowly died in France. I felt like I was beyond help, beyond salvation. The devil came to corrupt my thoughts, to make them bitter and confused. He came and snuffed out my light with his wicked mind games and he took away my fervour, as if it was his to take.

I fought him. I fought hard. I kept my family as safe as I could, and even when he forced his way into my home, he never completely broke through the barriers, as hard as he tried. I was a non-believer in the normal sense, so I had to fight the fight on earth without an established faith and it was exhausting. If I'd had the church…somewhere to go, I could have dealt with it all as I had always dealt with things in the past. Instead I was alone and very vulnerable.

Suddenly I had strange things happen to me. Burst tyres, rubbish bags going missing, nails on the garage floor, flowers ripped out of the garden, evidence of intruders when I wasn't at home…

The whole thing shook me up, but no more so than the trips I took on my own without my man at my side.

On the first occasion, Jake was in England, waiting for us to get home so that we could spend the week together. I had already input the destination into my Sat-Nav, so when he called to see if we were okay, he said, "Where are you now?"

"Uhm, not sure. I've just gone past that strange blue building on the right."

A pause

"What strange blue building?"

A pause.

"What road are you on?"

"I have no idea."

"Look at the Sat Nav. It tells you the road number."

"Oh, okay, hang on…" I read it out.

"Why are you there?"

What's with the questions? I could tell by his voice he was worried. The kids were in the back demanding a toilet break. "We're going to the ferry," I said with caution.

"You're on the wrong road, darling. You're way-off course. You're practically on the other side of France."

No! No more! "What do I do?"

At home he was looking at the map. It turned out I had inputted the wrong ferry terminal into my TomTom and added two more hours to my journey. "Luckily, you're coming up to a major junction, which will bring you back to where you need to be."

"I'm never that lucky!"

"Well, you're lucky now! If you'd passed it, you would have had to have continued for two more hours up the wrong AutoRoute."

"Thank God, then!"

On the next trip, I arrived at St. Malo port in good time. I had just completed a six hour journey up the motorway and I was exhausted from driving nonstop. The kids were cranky and my leg was aching from sitting still for so long. I needed more than anything to stretch and be quiet for a while, when to the children's delight, we found a McDonalds; its brightly lit logo like a beacon in the darkness.

As I watched the kids munch through their happy meal, I took out my ticket and looked at my watch. It was 9pm. My eyes went to the boarding time and it was only then I realised the ferry I'd booked was for ten o'clock in the morning, not ten at night. I couldn't believe how stupid I'd been. I was normally meticulous when travelling. *Everything was going wrong.*

Of course I admit liability. I was the one who'd booked the tickets. Surely it was no fault of the devil. Or was I right when I imagined him sniggering at me, enjoying my misery as I once more took to the road.

Jake was there for me on the phone. There were no ferries going from St. Malo until the next day, so I needed to drive up to Caen to catch the next boat leaving at midnight. It was pitch black and pouring with rain when we all got back into the car and as I strapped in the kids, I said, "Listen, darlings. Mummy has made a mistake and now we have to drive to another place, okay? Will you be good for mummy and keep quiet?"

"*D'accord, maman*," they said together.

As I drove with the rain belting down on the roof of the car, for the next two hours I prayed. Prayed we'd be delivered safely and that if it was the devil was trying to destroy me, that he would be chased away.

If I had put odds on a safe arrival, I would have said a 33-1 chance, but let's face it, when God's on our side, the odds are *always* in our favour.

The journey back to France was the worst since I was on my own with the children when I got severe food poisoning. It hit me when the ferry was an hour from docking. I couldn't move, let alone put on my leg so that I could get the children off the boat. I had no one to turn to for help and my phone was offline. The children were four-years old and I was doubled up on the bunk in agony, giving them instructions to get dressed.

"Put mummy's things in the bag," I croaked as the pain shot through my body like an electric charge. They did as they were told without a murmur. My head felt like it was going to drop off my shoulders, and when all I wanted to do was to go to sleep, the ship's tannoy blared for everyone to disembark. They were giving us five minutes and I couldn't move a muscle. Finally I gave myself over to the help of the crew. "Tom, I want you to be a big boy and go outside the cabin and see if you can find someone. Can you do that for mummy, baby?"

He didn't bat an eyelid. "Okay." He was so brave but frankly by then, he was used to going down that corridor. I watched him leave as Charlotte sat next to me sucking her thumb and stroking my hair. They were both as cool as cucumbers and I couldn't have loved them more.

Five minutes later, a crew member arrived with Tom in pursuit. I was taken in a wheelchair to the infirmary and while they wheeled me, someone else collected all my things and brought along the children with their little rucksacks fixed to their backs.

The ferry had docked. Everyone was getting off as my little Scenic was left all alone in a parking bay. I was lying on the infirmary bed when Tom and Charlotte sat side by side on two chairs near the door.

The doctor spoke English. "We have to get you off the ferry now," she said.

I nearly laughed. "Good luck with that. I can't move, I can't walk, and I can't drive."

"I'm going to give you some powders. You will be okay in half an hour."

"Thank you, but please, can I just close my eyes for a little while? I've got a six hour journey ahead of me."

"Yes, alright."

"My kids?"

"They can sit there quietly," she said, "Go to sleep."

Before I shut my eyes, I heard Charlotte speak to Tom, "What will we do if Mummy dies?" she said.

"Don't worry, Charlotte," he answered in a serious tone. "We'll still have daddy!"

Listening to the doctor chuckling, I shook my head at my children's practical approach to my demise and drifted off to sleep.

Half an hour later I was back in my car.

I don't know how I made it home but I stopped several times so that I could close one eye while the other watched the children. I had made a point of pulling over where some play equipment kept them occupied, so they didn't mind. I can't remember what they ate on the journey, maybe some left-over sandwiches and chocolate but I was past the point of caring.

We'd survived. *Thank God*

Chapter 23

-One Stepping Stone Back-

When I got back, I phoned Jake. "I've had enough, I'm coming home."

"You can't, love. We can't afford to buy in England."

"We'll rent."

"It'll break us."

"We'll manage. How many hints do we need, Jake, before something bad happens? I can't do it any more, not on my own. It would be manageable if you were here, but you're working all the time now. Our life is out of control."

"All our money will go on rent. I don't want to work like this forever."

"We didn't plan on the shift in the economy. That wasn't our fault."

"We can wait it out."

"If I stay here, it will kill me. I'm coming home."

So I left and we put the house up for sale.

Jake will probably deny it, but it took him five years before he forgave me for giving up on France. It was his dream and I ruined it and that put a wedge between us that had never existed before.

He found us a bungalow in a little village called Wrington, just below Bristol. How we ended up in that part of the world was anyone's guess. We could have gone anywhere, but that area seemed to beckon us.

The first day we moved in, I enrolled the kids in school. Even though we weren't villagers in the traditional sense, we were welcomed because Tom and Charlotte were bilingual and the headmistress at the time liked the idea of having bilingual twins in school. It was a social thing.

I had no idea how depressed I was. I put on a brave show and tried to adjust to our new life, even though, beneath my cheerful facade, I felt like I was sinking into some dark, foreboding place. I made new friends and the children settled in very well. They were popular in school, especially Charlotte. At a parent/teacher's meeting, her teacher told me Charlotte treated school like one big social occasion. I wasn't surprised. She was tall for her age with long blond hair and she had the cheeriest of dispositions.

Then one day the phone rang. The house in France had been burgled.

-Daily Disasters-

Since I'd left in a hurry, I forgot to bring back my precious ornaments. We owned a beautiful pair of art deco candlesticks in the shape of two ladies dressed in clinging gowns of brass. We'd picked them up from an antique fair years before and paid a lot of money for them. We also had a gorgeous silver teapot set on its own silver tray, given to us by Jake's parents. Much to my regret for leaving them in France when I should have brought them back with me, they were taken and we never saw them again!

I thought of the burglary as a personal violation, crushing me at a time when all my spirit was being sucked out of my body.

We decided there must have been two lots of intruders. One was the opportunists who broke in and battered down the doors looking for money and the other who'd come along afterwards, taking the fine pieces we had dotted around the place. We couldn't prove that, of course, but it also crossed our minds people would be thinking we'd staged the robbery for an insurance claim. But honestly, we weren't that well insured!

We were given some satisfaction two years later, when the gendarmerie caught the burglars by chance after they discovered our TV in a house nearby. The two men had worked on our vineyard and had taken the opportunity to rob our house. All they got was one year community service.

Two weeks after the robbery, another phone call came. The house had been flooded. The estate agent had gone in with some buyers and found water running through the ceiling to the rooms below. The house and our furniture were ruined.

Jake took time off work to get things fixed up. He took his parents with him to help and they brought some of our furniture home in a trailer towed behind

Jake's pick-up. But the weight of the cargo burned out the engine of the Shogun and they got stuck on the motorway. The vehicle and all our possessions had to be taken to a garage and Jake hired a car to get his parents back.

On the journey over he had tried to save cost by cutting down on breakdown insurance so we didn't have enough cover and had to pay for the car hire ourselves. In the meantime, the garage agreed to look at fixing the car, storing the trailer on site for a huge 500 Euros fee. It turned out the shogun was a write-off. We could either pay 8,000 Euros for a new engine or come and get it as it was.

We had no choice. We sold our caravan to raise the money to get everything back. Jake along with our amazing friend Dave Dear, went over to bring it all back to England.

Ironically, when they pulled the trailer up onto our drive, the back wheel dropped off and rolled away, as if it was saying, *I've had it. No more pulling for me.*

I knew exactly how it felt.

END OF PART 2

PART 3

When life gets us down, when everything is in darkness, it's hard to see the good things that happen, perhaps because we're overly focused on the bad. Why do we do that? Why can't every day be filled with hope and joy? I'm forever optimistic I will find that. That we all will one day. Without hope in something better, I ask you, what's the point?

My mother used to say, 'Heaven is where we go when we die and that hell is right here on earth'. I guess I've been tuned to feeling that way too but how about the good stuff? How about the moments of pleasure we all experience at least once. That's not hell, is it?

I am assured by the people who have introduced me to the faith, that one day all who follow Jesus will find paradise when they pass over to spend eternity with the Lord.

I have put all my trust and faith in God but I am more than aware there are people out there who don't believe and think us Christians are all deluded. But to them I say with a smile: play your lottery and good luck with hell on earth, because without Him, you'll never find Heaven as sweetly as I.

Wendy

Chapter 24

-Searching for God-

WE HAD TO MOVE ON. *Not by choice.* The last thing we wanted was to upset our lives again, but we were left with no option when our landlord put the bungalow on the market. He gave us six months to find somewhere else or purchase it ourselves but we were in no position to buy.

That same weekend four viewers arrived on a Saturday afternoon. We had already gone through so much disruption that I felt violated by them wandering around, looking at our things. I was starting to think everyone was against me. The whole human species was trying to take me down and trample all over me.

When the agents phoned on Sunday to set up another viewing, they were apologetic. "I'm sorry, Wendy. It's in the lease. You are obliged to show around perspective buyers."

"Fine!" I hung up. I was getting sick of being pushed around. By the time the viewers pulled up on the drive, I decided I was going to tell them to come back some other time and slam the door in their face. But when I saw a young couple standing there with their little girl, I sighed and opened the door wider. "Come in." As they stepped into the hall they offered their apologies and my hardened heart dissolved to a mushy pulp. "Charlotte," I called. "You've got a visitor."

They both came charging though the house. Tom saw it was a girl and went off again in a huff, but Charlotte took the little girl by the hand, leading her off to her room to play. "She'll look after her, if you want some space to look around," I said.

The next day I started searching for somewhere else to live. I needed to get us out of that house before I went completely mad.

-Dying of Depression-

Jake and I had become distant. We still loved each other deeply – how could we not after everything we'd been through together – but now I felt he resented me for coming home, for being the one who had created all the havoc after leaving the house in France and for spending all our available cash on rent. The thought of losing him was a final push into depression.

Then one day when we were driving back from Weston-Super-Mare through Congresbury, I saw a bungalow. *To Rent*, it said. I screamed and Jake slowed down. "That's it. That's the one we're going to live in. I just *know* it." I tapped the agent's number into my phone and pinned it to my ear. "I'm ringing about the bungalow in Congresbury."

"Sorry, it's been leased. The new tenants are moving in on Monday."

I sunk down into my seat and hung up. *What did I know?* Nothing was working out. *Nothing!*

At 11.00 on Monday morning, the agent called. "The new tenants have pulled out. He's just had a huge tax bill."

I wanted to feel sorry for him, but I couldn't. "We'll take it."

"Don't you want to see it first?"

I laughed. "If you want me to see it, I will."

We moved in the following week and enrolled the kids into Congresbury primary school, starting life anew.

Jake and I never got back to that place when we were blissfully happy, but we stayed together, faithful and true. I carried on with my writing and he kept on working. And even though we struggled, I always knew we had a love that could never be broken.

I kept potential friends at arm's length, preferring to be on my own rather than having to face new friendships which would inevitably turn sour. I became part of village life without a husband at my side and I guess many of them wondered about me. *Was I married? Why was I alone so much? Where's the husband?* If I was being gossiped about, it wouldn't have surprised me at that point.

-Perfect Potential-

I threw myself into my writing, hoping for a break into traditional publishing. One day I was looking at one of the kid's biology statues (The ones where the innards come out and you have to put them back in again in the right place). I looked at its face and thought, why hasn't someone written about creatures that looked like men with no skin, with a skull-like face? *It would make a great movie.* There began my new novel, 'The Perfects'

During my research I became very active on-line. My name was known around the cyber planet; in writing circles and forums. The internet was a new way of existing, with faceless friends who could be shut off with a click of a key. *Perfect!*

For a time I became a recluse and, if it hadn't have been for the children with their activities, I wouldn't have thought twice about locking the door and hiding within four walls until my life was over. Sooner rather than later.

I wrote three novels in as many years and when the publishing houses didn't come knocking on my door, I turned to self-publishing and put them up on Amazon. I mentored a young writers group in BookRix.com and while I helped the youngsters learn the craft, I kept growing, learning techniques and developing my own voice. I knew I was a good writer, but I couldn't convince agents and publishers to sign me up. It was one hard slog.

Then I fell and broke my hip.

The situation wasn't ideal for Jake when I went off to hospital. I felt he resented me even more by adding further disruption to our lives. He brought in his mother to care for the children but she was getting on and not up to looking after two rowdy kids. Especially ours!

I was kept in for two weeks. During visits, Jake kept his distance by sitting at the bottom of the bed, growling at me since I had once again given him a problem that made life even more difficult. It was a far cry from that day ten-years before when he walked into my room and saved my life. *No*, Jake had had enough and it was all my fault!

When the doctors X-rayed my hip, they found a sinus in the stump of my leg filled with the MRSA bug. If they operated, they said, they were worried they would disturb the sinus and infect the hip. If that happened, they wouldn't be able to stop it going through my body and if *that* happened…lights out.

Instead, he decided it would be better not to operate and allow my hip to heal naturally. It would take four months and I would have to confine myself to a wheelchair. From that moment on, I never wore an artificial leg again.

After two weeks I went home to start healing. I just wanting to get on with life and put the whole sorry episode behind me.

Life was a bomb. I'd had enough.

And then I met a girl.

Chapter 25

-Confirming Trinity-

I HAVE OFTEN CONSIDERED how a single encounter serves to connect people to form a physical and spiritual network. I'd had no connection to Jake on the day we met, until God's heavenly mesh brought us together. It was a fateful moment, one that had an enormous impact on my life, *and his*, and also the lives of the people connected to us. Had we not met, he wouldn't have saved me that day in hospital (obviously!). If I had died, we wouldn't have married; Tom and Charlotte wouldn't exist; I wouldn't have written this book; I wouldn't have lived in France; and without God's net plan, I wouldn't have met Avril, the woman who was instrumental in connecting me to Jesus.

When Avril guided me to Clevedon Baptist Church that day and I heard The Rev. Phil Hughes preaching the trinity, my whole life changed; Jake's life changed; and my children's lives changed. God used her to direct me to a place that would save me, mentally, socially, spiritually and even physically and that was big. *Really* big!

Sheila became my church mentor, helping me to face the challenges of being a baby Christian.

It began the day she came to my house, after my first visit to church. She spoke in a way that was true and heartfelt and I admired her so much. She was calm and serene, listening to my story without judgement. She told me about the devil and how he would cunningly work to stop me from getting to God and that when I felt he was there, I should say 'get behind me Satan' and he would leave.

Sheila amazed me with her knowledge of the Bible and her experiences. I thought of her as a special gift to me. She listened to my testimony that morning and wanted to offer me a passage from the Bible that was on her mind. She couldn't remember where it was but when she opened the book, the page fell to the right spot.

Now I call *Psalm 139* 'my Psalm', because the following day when Avril rang she said, 'You should read Psalm 139. You'll like it.' What other sign did I need? The piece that struck me most was the part that said *He* knew me when I was growing in the womb, long before I was born into the world. But mostly I was struck by the realisation that He'd been walking with me my whole life. It was a revelation for which I cried many tears, thinking about God being there all that time, carrying me when I didn't even know it. *Or did I?*

Unfortunately for my new friends in church, I didn't arrive quietly. I had so many emotions swirling around my head, so many questions, so many of my own thoughts that challenged theirs, I kept them all on their toes.

Sometimes I wondered if some of the church members thought my transition into the hands of God was all too quick to be true. They didn't know my past. They couldn't have known that God had been calling me from a very young age, nor that I had been searching for spiritual enlightenment all my life, that I had been searching...for *something*.

But despite anyone's doubts to my authenticity, I *had* hit the top target. I was totally in love with God and I wanted to shout it from the rooftops.

I wanted to cry out 'Bring it on.

I wanted to know everything.'

-Baby Steps-

After the initial introduction, I attended church each week and at every service I cried. I cried about my past life, I mourned the loss of the times I could have worshipped Him and how my life could have made more sense if I'd only realised He was there.

Jane, one of my dear friends and a long serving church leader, took me to one side after one service where I had sobbed all the way through. She asked me if I believed in God.

I frowned through my tears, and wondered why she was asking me that. "Yes, of course I do."

"Do you believe in Jesus?"

I hesitated. "That's where I have a bit of a mental block," I said. "I believe Jesus existed, but I can't get my head around him being the Son of God. I'm trying, but the whole thing eludes me. I can't pretend to believe in something. Maybe I should just stick with God."

"But you can only get to God through Jesus," she said.

I didn't believe that and I told her so. "I feel so close to God. I can't understand what you're saying."

"I've got a cd. I'll lend it to you. You can decide for yourself."

Then God spoke to me.

The day Jane gave me her cd, I took it home and realised it was the exact one that Sheila had given me, which I still hadn't got around to listening to. Only weeks before, I'd realised that if I opened my heart I could hear *Him* speak to me, offering guidance through words in my daily prayer book and the Bible.

I was on a journey, on a road to heavenly freedom, but one particular day, it was a lot more than that.

I'd just taken a call from France. My best friend, Celine, had incurable cancer and she was dying. 'For God's sake,' I cried. How many more will You take? How many more lives will You crush? She had two young children, one of them Charlotte's best friend. When I left her she was fine. She was only mid-thirties. *FOR GOD'S SAKE!*

In my misery, thinking about my darling friend and her suffering, I pulled out two black bags filled with laundry that needed ironing and decided to do the lot. I set up the board in the front room and took out the cd Jane and Sheila had given me, angrily shoving it into the slot.

The speaker was enigmatic, driven and faithful and his words hit many chords. Then, amid his dialogue, he said, '*I can't cure the cancer.*'

I stopped the iron running along the collar of a shirt and I did a double take. I shrugged and snarled

"Why not?" I spat as I continued to press the clothes with a heavy hand and a heavy heart. As the voice on the cd droned on, my thoughts drifted to Celine, lying in hospital waiting to die.

'*I can't cure the cancer,*' the voice on the cd shouted.

I stopped and looked around me. Was he speaking to me? Was I going crazy? I decided I was and carried on ironing.

'*I can't cure the cancer,*' the voice shouted at me for a third and final time.

I needed no more hints. God had spoken to me and the message was clear. *He couldn't cure the cancer.* I sobbed then for my beautiful friend who was going to die despite my desperate prayers.

Celine Garineau died in August that year in 2012 and I cried for three days. I couldn't go over to France for the funeral but all the mums from the school in St. Ciers put my name on the flowers, offering them as a tribute to a wonderful and very special woman.

That same day, as I ironed, I wrestled with my point about Jesus…Could he really have been the Son of God? Then, in a heartbeat, I accepted him. I just decided without any further ado that there was no point in fighting it and that I should give myself over to *Him* and accept Jesus as the Saviour, just as Phil had explained when he told the story of the trinity.

So that's what I did. I decided to follow Jesus and from that day on, my life has been *super* enriched.

Chapter 26

-Talking to God-

AS MY SPIRITUAL SIDE became more enhanced, I got down to business and began to pray every day. Many strange things happened as a result of me concentrating on receiving God's word and why Sheila told me to keep a journal from the very beginning.

At the onset of my belief in God, I was a crazy person. I wanted to shout about my new found faith from the rooftops. I felt liberated in a way I had never felt before and at last there was someone/something I could put all my trust into.

Avril was the one who accepted the excitement I felt about the revelations God offered me each day. I would ring her to tell her what had just happened, 'Isn't that amazing?' I'd shriek, whereupon she agreed it was and allowed me to rant joyously. At one point I wondered if everyone close to Avril had serious doubts

about me. She was spreading the good news about 'Wendy coming to the faith', explaining how excited I was to finally arrive home and how I wanted more and more and more…

There were perhaps some who were wary of that sort of quick transition. It had happened at the snap of two fingers, so how could anyone expect to believe everything I claimed was true? I could have been an imposter planning to defraud a girl who seemed to trust everyone. Perhaps the whole episode wasn't ringing true to them. They may have thought people turning to God like that didn't happen every day. Yes, they accepted me in good faith on the surface, but beneath their smiles and handshakes, perhaps there was a small amount of doubt lingering.

Then I got stuck in the church lift.

-Elevate Egos-

My fated companion was a lovely girl called Rachael, whose baby sat patiently in his pushchair while we discussed our plight of being trapped in the lift. We became sisters in arms, forced together by an uncontrollable event, while she offered me water from her baby's bottle. It had only been a few minutes so I told her it wasn't necessary. 'Feed the baby…' *Women and children first.*

We were stuck between floors and outside everyone was frantic. They couldn't identify who the trappees were, and were no doubt wondering about our physical health and mental capacity to deal with such a trauma.

Personally, I couldn't have cared less. I had been in a lot worse positions in my life, and I had my eternal faith in God who would surely work His magic and have us rescued soon enough.

Half an hour later, I was sitting on the floor of the elevator when the doors opened. Everyone was there; the church secretary; the security guy; a few onlookers and the two pastors who had been praying only minutes before for God to save the people trapped in the lift. No one knew it was me inside until the doors slid open. Someone came in to hoist me off the floor and as I was placed in a standing position I regarded some of their faces as they looked at me with strange expressions.

I laughed as I exited and shook hands with my rescuers as they told me that in the whole of the church's history that elevator hadn't once broken down. I mean *never*! It was the first time and inside was me, the woman who had just miraculously found the faith and joined their church in a heartbeat.

The following week I was presented with flowers for being so good about the whole unfortunate incident. A card was attached, which spoke of their regret and in it a verse: *Isaiah 41v13 "For I am the Lord, your God, who takes hold of your right hand and says to you, do not fear. I will help you."*

I accepted their attempt to reach out to me. I knew it would be a matter of time before they accepted me as a part of the family. I knew God would see to that. I just didn't know he would take such drastic action by getting me trapped in the lift.

My prayer that morning was *Psalm 91*, themed as God's protection in the midst of danger.

Psalm 91:1 He who dwells in the shelter of the Most High will rest in the shadow of the Almighty.

I thought it was quite apt.

Chapter 27

-A Divine Encounter-

I WAS WALKING ON CLOUDS. Suddenly everything was going right in my life. My head became clear of dismal thoughts and resentment and my heart and mind became open to everything that came my way. I shouted my new found faith from the rooftops and I wanted everyone to be as happy as me. I couldn't get enough. I attended church twice every Sunday, in the morning and evening, I went to prayer group and to anything that was on in the week I could attend. And it still wasn't enough. It was like a terrible thirst, quenched only by a liaison with God.

I'd shocked myself. I never thought I would become a follower. In fact it was only a year before when I told dad off for sending me emails containing religious stuff. I was *that* anti-Christianity!

Avril became my earthly guide. I called her my saviour, but she wouldn't accept the compliment. It's not about me," she'd say. "God is using me to get to you. I am merely the messenger." Avril taught me how to use the Bible, how to absorb the Word of God and use it in my daily life. She connected me to everything and whilst I grew, she revelled in the message God was giving us when so many strange things happened.

I complained a lot. "Where can I go to pray every day?" I needed to speak to him *every day*. Sunday wasn't enough. "Give me more."

"You can pray at home," Sheila said. "And keep a journal, you may want to look back on these times one day and see how far you've travelled."

When I walked around my house looking for a place that felt special enough for me to sit and talk to God, I couldn't find a spot that warmed me. So I went on-line and ordered a statue of Jesus so that I could create a focal point; my own little church.

Everyone frowned when I told them, but I argued, "Who wants to sit in a living room without a fireplace to keep them warm?" The statue sustained me (It still does) and no attempt at persuading me otherwise worked. He was mine and he was there to stay. *Just like God.*

One day I felt like I wanted to get deeper in prayer. I thought if I could literally close out all the noise and interruptions in my life, I could develop an even closer relationship with God.

Suddenly, a thought popped into my head. *'Go to St. Andrews church.'*

It was only ten in the morning in the middle of the week, but the voice was too strong for me to ignore. God wanted me to go to the church in our village. I grabbed my keys and left, got into my car and drove in the rain to St. Andrews church next to the school.

I'd been there before, but only as a parent supporting the school. Now I was there in a different capacity. I was now a member of that institution called 'The Church' and I didn't have to feel guilty or afraid to go inside.

I was surprised to find it open.

There was no one around when I walked to the little prayer chapel at the far side. I lit a candle, placed a coin in the box, and sat down as I waited for whatever God had in mind to happen. I thought it might have been Matt, the vicar, who would appear. Maybe God wants me to have a talk with him about my new-found faith.

A lady came in. She didn't speak. She simply came into the chapel, lit a candle and then went and sat in the main church. That's when I realised I was out of my mind. God wasn't speaking to me. I was an idiot.

I laughed at myself for being such a fool. It was time to leave. I stood up. Then a thought came into my head

'*Go speak to that lady.*'

What? No, I'm not speaking to that lady. I don't know her and she'll think I'm mental. I walked down the aisle towards the entrance.

'*Go speak to that lady.*'

I almost guffawed. *Voices in my head. That's all this is. It's not God.* I turned a corner and walked toward the door.

'*Go speak to that lady.*'

I needed to get out. There was no way I was going to go up to a perfect stranger and announce that God was speaking to me. I pulled the handle of the heavy door and stepped outside. The rain had stopped and the sun was shining.

Then I fell over.

I was right outside the door, sitting in a puddle. I couldn't get up on my own and there was no one around to help me...no one except the lady in the church!

-Falling for Soul Gym-

I reached up and pushed the door ajar. "Hello!?" I called. "Can you help me?" I saw her rush out. "I'm sorry," I said, "I've fallen over and I can't get up."

She had a nice face and I was glad of her help when she pulled me to my feet. "Are you hurt?" she asked.

I thought about it for a second. "Actually, no, I'm not."

"I'll help you to your car."

"Thank you." I flicked the remote and sat down on the seat behind the wheel.

"My name's Veronica," she said.

I pondered the time only an hour before. "You'll think I'm mad," I said "but I had an overwhelming feeling I should come to church this morning. I don't normally come here. I go to Clevedon Baptist."

"Really? That's strange, because I don't normally come at this time. I forgot my umbrella this morning, so I came back for it. I decided to stay and have a little prayer."

I thought back to my prayers that morning and how I couldn't get a connection with God with all the noise and disruptions, and how I wanted more than anything to get deeper in prayer. "I couldn't concentrate at home and wanted to find somewhere peaceful to pray."

"You should come to Soul gym."

"Sole what?"

"*Soul* gym. It's a gathering we have once a month with Matt, to learn how to get deeper in prayer through meditation. You may enjoy it."

"That sounds good. Maybe I will."

When I got back, I rang Avril. "Have you ever heard of soul gym?"

She gasped. "I've been wanting to go to that for so long, but never found the time. Shall we go?"

"I think we should."

On our first morning of soul gym, Tina came too and I think we were all expecting a miracle, since it was God who had sent us there. Instead, it began a relationship with St. Andrews Church I may never have had if I hadn't have fallen over and met Veronica that day.

I never saw her again, until I met her by chance two years later at a church meeting. She remembered the occasion but she was as surprised as everyone else at how she had been used by God to help me find soul gym.

Secondary school

Avril

My family

Growing up

Chapter 28

-Pennies from Heaven-

I CAN'T REMEMBER the amount of times in my life I'd prayed to win the lottery, but the day I handed myself over to God I decided to stop.

I had always been a gambler in life, certainly nothing serious; only enjoying a little flutter now and again, like my mother who liked to back the horses with a few pennies, but after I made a commitment to Jesus, striving to be more like Him, I wanted to do it right.

I haven't bought a lottery ticket since and I can utterly recommend it.

At the time, our finances were a real struggle, since we hadn't managed to sell the house in France. But as soon as I stopped wishing for a windfall or gambling on uncertainties and accepting that God would provide if I trusted Him, we sold it. In the meantime we kept receiving unexpected money from all quarters, on tax refunds and pensions, some of my debts were written off and I was awarded back-dated disability benefits.

Suddenly everything had changed, because I stopped wishing for the thing that would probably add to our downfall rather than improve it. In the same way many lottery winner's lives are made worse with sudden, ridiculous amounts of monetary wealth.

I recall a special occasion when I had to attend a tribunal in Bristol, to get back the disability benefit the government had taken off me. It was that time in 2013, when they'd contracted a French company to test everyone for their eligibility to receive Incapacity Benefit. Many people in wheelchairs suddenly lost their income, mothers with disabled children lost their income and people who genuinely couldn't earn a living due to serious health issues lost their income. I was one of them. I was deemed fit for work despite my situation and that, in the worst case scenario, I was told I could go out to work in a wheelchair, seeing as I had two arms to propel myself.

My case, along with several million others, went to tribunal to claim back the money they'd taken off us.

When I arrived in Bristol for my hearing, I took the advice of the courts and parked in a designated multi-story car park. I was alone when I came out of the building on crutches and asked for directions to the tribunal. A man in a white van thrust his arm out of the window and pointed north, up a steep hill that even cars struggled to climb. "I can't get up there," I said. I wondered for a moment if he'd offer me a lift, but when he took a big bite from his cheese baguette, I took that as a no.

Only five minutes before, a man in the car park had let a heavy fire door shut in my face because he was in such a hurry, so I was beginning to wonder if it was just going to be a bad day.

Outside the entrance to the car park, as I reflected on life and the story in the bible about the Good Samaritan, I leaned up against a wall to phone for help. I was praying when a lady went past me. She turned to look at my sorry face, but she carried on walking. When she arrived at her car, parked a few meters along the side of the road, she turned and shouted "Are you okay?"

I shook my head. "I have to be in court in ten minutes and I can't get up the hill."

Without hesitation she said, "I'll take you,"

"Really?" *No way!* I thought. *It couldn't be that easy!*

She opened her car door and helped me into the passenger seat. As she started up the ignition she said, "I don't normally park here but I had time to do a bit of shopping before work. I remember thinking how lucky I was to find a free parking space."

Lucky?

"I'm glad you did," I said. We introduced ourselves as she drove me up the hill. "I think you are my Good Samaritan," I said. "I was praying for help when you came along. God gave you to me."

I waited for her to laugh at my comment but, instead, she told me she was a Christian. I gasped when she opened the glove compartment to show me a hand carved wooden cross, as if she wanted to prove her testimony. She was also a member of AA, just like my dad.

Despite feeling miserable and helpless only seconds before, I suddenly felt lifted, realising God was in charge, and that he had sent an angel to watch over me.

I went on to win my case. *Naturally!*

-Cold Calling-

Another time I got one of those annoying cold calls.

"Can I interest you in buying a ticket for the postcode lottery?" the voice said.

Normally I would politely decline and hang up (okay, so I'm not *always* polite) but now he'd mentioned the magic word, 'lottery'!

As he rambled on doing the hard sell, I considered it for a moment but then I remembered what I had promised God. "No can do, sorry. I'm a Christian and I don't gamble anymore."

"Well, that's okay, because some of the money goes to charity. You can't get any more Christian than that."

Yeah right!

I hesitated… "Nope, you can't talk me into it. Can't gamble sorry….but wait, I'll ask my husband. He might have a go." I figured Jake could buy one, since he didn't believe in God. He was just outside the back door. "Jake…Do you want to buy a ticket off this guy?"

"No."

I spoke into the phone "He doesn't want one either."

"Are you sure I can't persuade you?"

Pause. *Would it hurt?* "No, you can't. Sorry!" I hung up and took a glance at my little statue of Jesus and said. "I hope you appreciated that."

"What…?" called Jake from outside the back door.

"Nothing!" I yelled. "I'm just talking to Jesus."

The next morning I got a letter in the post. The government had been trying to get tax off me for when I lived in France. I'd been fighting against it for months. The letter said, it was letting the matter go.

My reward for not gambling was worth five figures.

-Bingo and Blessings-

My small desire to gamble was tested once again last year when I went with the family for a caravan holiday in Woolacombe bay. We were on a huge camp site where in the evenings they ran bingo sessions. I decided to have a go, telling myself that it was just a game, and nothing serious! *God wouldn't mind!*

When I arrived, the room was very crowded with many boisterous children screaming at a man on stage, dressed as a beach ball.

After I was told to go up to the front to buy my tickets, all guilty thoughts left me as I balanced on two sticks and made my way through the crowd. But, just as I got there the ticket man was called away by an agitated lady who had lost her child. He went off with her, leaving the booth empty.

I've been an amputee for fifteen years now, so I have long got over the staring factor, but as I stood there alone feeling everyone was watching me, I felt so uncomfortable, I decided to leave.

There's one thing I've discovered since falling in love with Jesus, you can't con him. I soon realised that it was God who had prevented me from breaking my promise and gambling again. It was Him who had made that little girl get momentarily lost and it was *Him* who had made the bingo man walk away, just so I couldn't get my hands on those tickets.

When I got home, a letter was waiting for me from my pension company. Apparently they hadn't been paying me enough. My account had been credited with £1000, paid in on the day after I walked away from temptation.

Chapter 29

-Many Miracles-

WITH SO MANY AMAZING events logged in my journal, I couldn't begin to write about them all. After all, how much paper is there in the world? *However*...I have to tell you about my visit to the New Word Alive conference in North Wales in 2013.

Avril had mentioned the annual event many times, trying to encourage me to book a chalet and go but I was dismissive of her hints. Pontins didn't hold such good memories for me, since I'd gone there once when I was kid and my father was drunk out of his mind each day. The one principle I'd lived by when dealing with my past, was to move on and not go there again, but God had other ideas.

It was January. All my Christian friends were booked on the holiday to NWA, except me. I just wasn't interested. *There was the cost*...Besides, I'd lost the brochure Avril had given me so I didn't know anything about it. I didn't *want* to know anything about it.

One morning I was rummaging through some filing, when the stack of papers I held on my lap dropped to the floor. I bent down and gathered them up, and *naturally* I pushed them inside a cupboard and shut the door. When I moved over to the other side of the room, there on the floor, right in my path, was the leaflet for NWA staring right at me.

I picked it up and rang Avril. "I've just found the leaflet for New Word Alive," I said. "Do you think it's a sign?"

"Definitely! God wants you to go."

"I doubt if they'll have anything available at this late stage," I said.

"You won't know unless you make the call."

I rang the booking line. "I don't suppose you've got a chalet for three? It has to be on the ground floor, with a disabled shower and close to the amenities?"

I knew she'd laugh. "NWA gets booked up a year in advance. I doubt if we have anything to meet your specifications but I'll have a look."

I was doodling on my still blank note pad. I didn't stand a chance but now I was feeling quite keen to go.

She came back on the phone. "That's weird," she said.

"What is?"

I've got one chalet left. It's on the ground floor, it's got a disabled shower and it's close to the amenities."

I chuckled. "Let's book that then," I said.

Across the table was an unopened letter addressed to Jake. He'd been given a lump sum from his pension people and it was more than enough to cover the cost of the holiday.

A week before we were about to depart for the New Word Alive conference I fell and broke my arm. I'd taken the most ridiculous fall, where I'd tripped over the door jam and fell flat on my face.

When Jake picked me up from hospital that evening with my arm in plaster, I was more than just a little miffed. "How am I going to get around? I can't walk on crutches and I can't use my artificial leg."

"You can use your wheelchair." He sounded like he'd already worked things out.

"How do I propel it?"

"Uhm…we could get you an electric one."

"We can't afford it. And what about New Word Alive? Now I won't be able to go."

"You'll find a way."

"No I won't," I sulked.

Avril rang. "I'll help. I can push you around in the wheelchair."

"I don't want to go in my wheelchair. I'll look like a dork. I thought I'd be going around on crutches. Besides, I can't drive now."

"We'll work it out. And I can drive you."

Despite everyone's upbeat attitude, I was angry. I had just spent a whole year praising God, worshipping Him, and believing in Him with my whole being. Why was he now turning his back on me by allowing me to break my arm? The whole episode didn't make sense.

-Baptised and Blessed-

My arm was still in plaster on the day of my baptism on 31-3-13, a poignantly placed palindrome and a date I shared with the celebration of the resurrection of Christ. *There was no better company!* The anger I felt about my broken arm had been long spent. I hadn't talked to God for two weeks, but I couldn't go any longer without Him in my life.

I shared the occasion with Tina and a chap called Bob. Our family and friends were there to watch us offer our testimonies before we were fully immersed in a baptism pool. I would never have predicted going through the baptism ritual. I normally hated ceremonies, especially ones that involved me and I was outspoken about not being carried away on a tide of rules and disciplines. I wanted it to be my choice alone and not just done for the benefit of the church or to please others. But there I was, wanting to give myself completely, holding nothing back and thanking Him for sticking around when I had spent a lifetime denying His existence.

To me, getting baptised was a demonstration of my faith. It was a promise to God that I was about to devote my life to worshipping Him and accepting him as the Father. It was a confirmed spiritual connection.

The following day Tina and I said we both felt His arms around us when we all took off to Pontins in North Wales. When we pulled up at the site, I knew straight away why God had allowed me to fall and break my arm. It wasn't because He wanted to punish me or to get my attention…It wasn't because He wanted me to realise He was with me every minute of every day and it wasn't because He cared about me deeply and that He wanted me to testify to His presence.

I'd had no comprehension of the expanse of the place, so if I'd arrived with just my crutches to get around, I would never have made the course. It turned out I *had to* use my wheelchair, even if I didn't want to. Apart from the notion that I was being looked after, the best part was realising God knew it long before me.

People say, 'funny how things turn out' but the way I see it, *things* turn out the way they do because -good or bad- everything's part of God's great plan. You may not like it and His methods may seem a little drastic; and there may be times when you can't make sense of it all, but for me, as I look back at the time I fell and lost my leg, I believe it all happened to enrich my life.

And It did!

Epilogue

-The Red Carpet-

IT RECENTLY OCCURRED TO ME that everything I've written about my life and the wonderful events that brought me to God may be hard for some people to accept. I mean I could be exaggerating, couldn't I? Or embellishing, as we call it in the literary world. Or perhaps I could be lying? Maybe I'm prone to fantasising about things because I was made crazy when I was a kid?

Well, if you think my past was crazy, or that you're finding it all a bit hard to believe, you may as well stop here and go read Jordan's bio, because it gets even crazier.

I wrote another book, 'The Song of the Underground', about a lost city beneath London. I thought of the idea when I saw a documentary about Victorian subterranean tunnels under the capital, a haven for explorers and underground enthusiasts. When

I completed the novel, I thought of it as my best work yet and I was sure I'd get picked up by an agent and publisher. But as usual with my life, things don't go as I expect them to, and that occasion was no exception.

Being active on-line, you get to meet people all over the world, faceless people, until they eventually come out and their avatar looks nothing like the person you'd imagined.

A lady called Valerie Byron held no such coyness. She was over sixty and beautiful and she had a past in the golden days of Hollywood that would make your hair curl. She wrote 'No Ordinary Woman', a title befitting such an enigmatic lady. The thing with Val, she liked to help everyone, but she mainly wanted to help me. She considered me to be a talented writer, far beyond the realms of the writing skills of most of the people we'd met on-line. Such a mentor was she, she got in touch with a friend of hers, legendary movie mogul, Budd Burton Moss. She prompted him to look at *The Song*, and suggested he and I could be a partnership made in heaven.

That's how I picked up a Hollywood manager, when he rang me one night and with his sharp American drawl he told me how excited he was about the project and that he hoped to find someone to option the script. "I haven't got a script," I said. "It's only in book form."

"Then write it, dear Wendy. Write it!"

Budd Burton Moss was old school, rising through his career years in the golden days of Hollywood. He placed Larry Hagman and Barbara Eden in the long running series *I Dream of Jeannie*, Elizabeth Montgomery in *Bewitched* and he made Mia Farrow's original deal for *Peyton Place* with 20th Century Fox, as well as Robert

Vaughn in *The Man from Uncle*. He got Dyan Cannon in the movie *Bob, Carol, Ted and Alice*, for which she received an Oscar nomination and he put Tom Bosley in *Happy Days*… Oh and Sydney Poitier was his best man! The list goes on, but there he was talking on the phone to little ol' Wendy in Congresbury!

Budd's dream was to get 'The Song of the Underground' produced as a movie, and maybe even picked up as a play on the West End. His first port of call was to his friend at Imagine Entertainment, Ron Howard, better known as Richie Cunningham in Happy Days. Ron passed it to his executive assistant, Anna Culp, since he was bogged down with movie projects for the next five years.

Anna took it to Universal who liked the premise but suggested the script should be changed before they'd consider it. Budd also took it to Warner Studios, who more or less said the same.

Since the people involved didn't want to pay for a professional screen writer, the project faded to a whisper and we still await that call.

No matter! As far as I was concerned, eight years before, I didn't even know I could write, but there I was in 2013 having my script placed on the desks of the three biggest studios in Hollywood. Strange but true!

Maybe someday my story will be up on the silver screen and if I live that long, there I'll be, balanced on two sticks, skipping down that red carpet for everyone to see.

Six months ago in 2014.

Jake and I both knew we belonged together and that the miraculous meeting we had twenty years before was meant for us to last forever.

Jake hated the house we were living in. He was grumpy and sad all the time, and always impatient with me and the children. He hated his life, and his reaction to that offered no comparison to the man I'd fallen in love with over twenty years before.

Last year, out of the blue, our landlords gave us notice as they needed to sell the house. I didn't want to leave Congresbury. I'd always said it was the one place I could call home and that if I left, they'd have to carry me out. But now we had no choice. We had to find a new place to live.

So I prayed.

I prayed to God to find us a house where we could be happy, but I was very specific about what I wanted. 'He won't give you things on demand,' someone told me, but I asked Him anyway. What did I have to lose?

I asked God for a bungalow with no steps, a large amount of storage, three bedrooms, a big garden and a kitchen with a non-slip floor. Most of all I prayed for a house that would make Jake happy, to bring him back from the place he was, so that we could love each other again.

Three months later a house popped up on Prime Location. It was a bungalow with lots of storage, no steps, four bedrooms, a big garden and a kitchen…with a non-slip floor…right next to the school…in a lovely part of Somerset, where I had once dreamed about living.

Just like the other time I rang up the agent. "We'll take it."

"Don't you want to see it first?"

I laughed. "If you want me to see it I shall, but we'll take it anyway"

Strangely -*or not so strangely*- the agent's computer system went down after I rang, so no one could ring up and make a counter-offer.

As far as I was concerned, God had it all planned. The house was ours. We've lived in Churchill ever since.

Today I watch Jake sitting outside in the garden with a smile on his face, looking out over the lawn to a stone walled barn; a place that reminds him of being in France. Now he's happy and he laughs a lot.

Thank God!

THE END
(For now)

A Little Bit of Wisdom
(not mine)

"You need to recognise the presence of the Holy Spirit within you and build a relationship with Him. He's not an 'it' or a 'thing' or an ethereal spirit that's beyond your reach. He is Christ's representative. He's willing to teach you what you don't know, and to remind you of all the things you so easily forget. And best of all, He will give you peace of mind and heart, regardless of what life throws at you."

"When you need an advisor because you're not sure what to do or where to go, the Holy Spirit is there to guide you. That means you must be sensitive when He highlights a particular Scripture you're reading, or plants a persistent thought or idea in your mind that won't go away, or speaks to you through a friend. You're not alone, unless you want to be. Just consult the counsellor within you."

Taken from the UCB daily read 2015

Me and Jake 2015

-A Final Note for Children of Alcoholics-

When my dad got sober I forgave him for everything and went forward with my life as best I could. I didn't want to carry emotional baggage. That was his life. I wanted to leave that all behind and begin my own.

I am thankful I came out of it with a smile on my face, my sanity intact and just a little bruised. I learned a lot about life's challenges and I believe it prepared me for the life I now lead. Throughout it all, I believe I stayed strong, never wanting to hurt anyone, adapting to life, making something of myself, and ultimately learning how to take everything thrown at me on the chin, to get up, brush myself down, deal with it, and move on.

I feel blessed to have been given the strength to do that. Many children of alcoholics go the other way, continuing with substance abuse as a way of dealing with the memories of their broken childhood, or worse still, repeating the abuse by marrying into a relationship based on alcohol.

To the kids I'd like to say, even if you don't believe in God, those of you who relate to some of the things I have experienced, whatever your parent did, don't let them take your whole life. If you can, I urge you to break free of the cycle and go write your own history. Most of all, forgive them if you can.

There are many self-help groups out there, but my preferences are Alanon, for the spouses of alcoholics, Alateen, for young adult children of alcoholics and a group on-line called ACOA for children of alcoholics in adulthood. They are all worthy and safe environments to speak to like-minded individuals and to take that first step into recovery.

There is also one group that does all of that and more, and that's church. Don't be frightened of it, because the place is full of people just like you.

Wendy

Novels by Wendy Reakes

Wendyreakes.com

Please leave feedback on Amazon. It really helps!